The Untold Journey of kioShiMa

The French Support – Unauthorized

Rina Cruz

ISBN: 9781779698872
Imprint: Telephasic Workshop
Copyright © 2024 Rina Cruz.
All Rights Reserved.

Contents

Prologue   **1**
The Rise of eSports   1

Chapter One: The Making of a Prodigy   **13**
Early Beginnings   13
Rise through the Amateur Ranks   18
The Big Break   24

Chapter Two: The French Shuffle and the Road to Success   **33**
The French Shuffle   33
Finding Stability with G2 Esports   39
The Majors and Major Disappointments   45

Chapter Three: Struggles and Overcoming Adversity   **53**
Personal and Team Challenges   53
The Journey to Redemption   61

Chapter Four: Legacy and Impact   **71**
kioShiMa's Influence on CS:GO   71
The Evolution of eSports in Europe   78
The Future of kioShiMa   84

Epilogue   **91**
The End of an Era   91
The Unseen Side of kioShiMa   98
The Future of eSports   105

Index   **113**

Prologue

The Rise of eSports

The Evolution of Competitive Gaming

The landscape of competitive gaming has undergone a dramatic transformation over the past few decades, evolving from humble beginnings into a global phenomenon that captivates millions. This evolution can be traced through several key phases, each marked by technological advancements, cultural shifts, and the emergence of organized competitions.

Early Beginnings

The roots of competitive gaming can be found in the late 1970s and early 1980s, with the advent of arcade games such as *Pong* and *Space Invaders*. These games not only introduced players to the concept of high scores but also laid the groundwork for competitive play. Players would gather in arcades, vying for the top spot on the leaderboard, creating a sense of community and rivalry.

The Rise of Home Consoles

The introduction of home consoles in the 1980s, such as the Atari 2600 and the Nintendo Entertainment System (NES), further democratized access to video games. This era saw the rise of multiplayer games, where friends could compete against one another in their living rooms. The concept of tournaments began to take shape, with events like the *Nintendo World Championships* in 1990 showcasing the competitive spirit of gaming on a larger stage.

The Internet Revolution

The late 1990s marked a pivotal moment in the evolution of competitive gaming with the rise of the internet. Online gaming platforms such as *Battle.net* and *GameSpy* allowed players to compete against others from around the world. This shift not only expanded the player base but also introduced new genres of games, such as real-time strategy (RTS) and first-person shooters (FPS), which became staples of competitive gaming.

The Birth of eSports

The term "eSports" began to gain traction in the early 2000s as organized competitions started to emerge. Games like *Counter-Strike*, *StarCraft*, and *Dota* attracted large audiences, both online and in-person. Major tournaments, such as the *World Cyber Games* and *Electronic Sports World Cup*, showcased the talents of top players and teams, establishing a framework for professional gaming.

The Mainstream Breakthrough

The 2010s witnessed a seismic shift in the perception of competitive gaming. With the rise of streaming platforms like *Twitch*, players could broadcast their gameplay to a global audience. This accessibility not only increased the visibility of eSports but also attracted sponsorships from major brands, further legitimizing the industry. The prize pools for tournaments skyrocketed, with events like The International for *Dota 2* offering millions of dollars to champions, solidifying the status of eSports as a viable career path.

Cultural and Social Impact

As competitive gaming continued to grow, it began to intersect with broader cultural movements. The rise of gaming as a spectator sport led to the establishment of dedicated eSports arenas, where fans could gather to watch their favorite teams compete live. Additionally, the increasing diversity of games and players contributed to a more inclusive gaming community, challenging stereotypes and promoting representation.

Challenges and Controversies

Despite its rapid growth, the evolution of competitive gaming has not been without challenges. Issues such as player burnout, mental health concerns, and controversies surrounding cheating and match-fixing have sparked discussions about the sustainability of the industry. Moreover, the struggle for recognition and legitimacy within the broader sports community remains an ongoing battle for eSports.

The Future of Competitive Gaming

Looking ahead, the future of competitive gaming appears bright. With advancements in technology, such as virtual reality (VR) and augmented reality (AR), the potential for immersive gaming experiences is limitless. Furthermore, the integration of eSports into educational institutions and the potential for Olympic inclusion could pave the way for even greater recognition and acceptance.

In conclusion, the evolution of competitive gaming reflects a dynamic interplay of technology, culture, and community. From its modest beginnings in arcades to its current status as a global phenomenon, competitive gaming has transformed the way we play, watch, and engage with video games. As we continue to witness this evolution, one thing remains clear: competitive gaming is here to stay, and its impact will only grow in the years to come.

The Emergence of Professional eSports

The emergence of professional eSports represents a seismic shift in the landscape of competitive gaming, transforming what was once a casual pastime into a formidable industry. This transformation can be traced back to the late 1990s and early 2000s, when competitive gaming began to gain traction, leading to the establishment of organized tournaments and professional teams. The convergence of technology, community engagement, and financial investment laid the groundwork for what we now recognize as professional eSports.

The Early Days of Competitive Gaming

In the late 20th century, video games began to evolve from solitary experiences into competitive events. Games like *Quake* and *StarCraft* emerged as front-runners in the competitive gaming scene. The first significant tournament, the *Red Annihilation* in 1997, showcased the potential for competitive play. Players from around the globe gathered to compete for a grand prize, marking the inception of organized eSports.

$$P = \frac{E}{T} \tag{1}$$

Where P is the level of professionalization, E represents the engagement of players and fans, and T is the time invested in competitive play. As the equation suggests, the more time players invested in honing their skills, the greater the engagement and, consequently, the level of professionalization.

The Role of Technology

The advancement of technology played a pivotal role in the emergence of professional eSports. High-speed internet connections allowed players to compete against one another in real-time, breaking geographical barriers. Streaming platforms like *Twitch* revolutionized how fans consumed content, enabling viewers to watch their favorite players and teams compete live. This accessibility fostered a community around competitive gaming, further solidifying its status as a legitimate sport.

The Rise of Sponsorship and Investment

As eSports gained popularity, businesses began to recognize its potential for marketing and branding. Sponsorship deals became commonplace, with companies eager to align themselves with successful teams and players. This influx of investment not only provided financial support for teams but also legitimized eSports in the eyes of the public.

For instance, in 2014, *Team SoloMid* secured a sponsorship deal worth $1 million with *Logitech*, highlighting the financial viability of professional eSports. Such sponsorships allowed teams to expand their operations, hire coaches, and invest in training facilities, further professionalizing the scene.

Establishment of Leagues and Tournaments

The establishment of structured leagues and tournaments marked a significant milestone in the evolution of professional eSports. Organizations like *ESL* and *Major League Gaming (MLG)* began organizing events that attracted thousands of participants and viewers. The *Dota 2 International*, launched in 2011, offered a prize pool of over $1 million, demonstrating the financial potential of professional gaming.

$$R = \frac{P}{N} \tag{2}$$

Where R is the revenue generated from a tournament, P is the prize pool, and N is the number of participants. This equation illustrates how larger prize pools can attract more participants, thereby increasing revenue opportunities for organizers.

The Cultural Shift

As professional eSports gained traction, a cultural shift began to take place. No longer viewed as mere entertainment for the socially awkward, competitive gaming started to be embraced by mainstream society. Major sporting events began to acknowledge eSports, with tournaments being held in prestigious venues such as the *Staples Center* in Los Angeles.

The recognition of eSports as a legitimate form of competition prompted discussions about its classification as a sport. While traditionalists debated the merits of eSports compared to physical sports, the undeniable skill and strategy involved in games like *Counter-Strike: Global Offensive* and *League of Legends* continued to draw in audiences.

The Future of Professional eSports

Looking ahead, the future of professional eSports appears bright. With an ever-growing audience, increased investment, and the potential for global tournaments, the landscape is ripe for further evolution. The rise of mobile gaming and the integration of virtual reality could introduce new dimensions to competitive play, attracting even more players and fans.

In conclusion, the emergence of professional eSports is a testament to the power of community, technology, and innovation. As we continue to witness the growth of this phenomenon, it is clear that professional eSports is not just a fleeting trend but a significant part of the cultural fabric of our time. The journey from casual gaming to a multi-billion dollar industry is a story of passion, perseverance, and the relentless pursuit of excellence.

The Growth of Counter-Strike: Global Offensive (CS:GO)

The evolution of competitive gaming has witnessed several pivotal moments, but few have been as significant as the rise of *Counter-Strike: Global Offensive* (CS:GO). Released in 2012, CS:GO not only revitalized the long-standing *Counter-Strike* franchise but also set a new standard for competitive gaming, becoming a cornerstone of the esports industry.

A New Era in First-Person Shooters

CS:GO emerged from the legacy of its predecessors, *Counter-Strike 1.6* and *Counter-Strike: Source*. The original *Counter-Strike* was a mod for *Half-Life* that introduced players to team-based gameplay, where strategy and skill were paramount. However, CS:GO brought with it a modernized engine, improved graphics, and refined gameplay mechanics. This new iteration retained the core essence of tactical team play while introducing new features such as:

- **Weapons and Economy System:** CS:GO introduced a more intricate economy system that rewarded players for their performance, thereby adding a layer of strategic depth. Players needed to manage their in-game finances carefully, deciding when to purchase weapons and equipment, which directly influenced their team's success.

- **Maps and Game Modes:** The game launched with a variety of maps, each designed to promote different styles of play. From the bomb defusal mode to hostage rescue scenarios, the diverse game modes catered to a broad audience, encouraging both casual and competitive play.

- **Competitive Matchmaking:** CS:GO pioneered a robust matchmaking system that allowed players to compete against others of similar skill levels. This feature not only made the game more accessible but also fostered a sense of community and rivalry among players.

The Role of Tournaments and Events

The growth of CS:GO can be attributed significantly to the establishment of professional tournaments and leagues. Events such as *ESL One*, *DreamHack*, and *Blast Premier* attracted thousands of fans, both in-person and online, creating a vibrant esports culture.

The introduction of the Major Championships, starting with the *DreamHack Major* in 2013, marked a turning point in the game's competitive landscape. These events offered substantial prize pools, often exceeding $1,000,000, and drew the best teams from around the world. The formula for success at these events hinged on the combination of individual skill, teamwork, and strategic depth, epitomized by teams like *Fnatic*, *SK Gaming*, and Astralis.

Community and Streaming Influence

The role of the community and streaming platforms such as *Twitch* cannot be overstated in the growth of CS:GO. The game's accessibility allowed a diverse range of players to engage with it, while streamers and content creators showcased their skills, strategies, and personalities, drawing in millions of viewers.

The rise of popular streamers like *Shroud* and *Ninja* helped to popularize CS:GO, making it a household name in gaming. Their gameplay not only entertained but also educated viewers on advanced techniques and strategies, further enriching the community knowledge base.

The Challenges of Growth

Despite its success, CS:GO faced significant challenges that threatened its growth trajectory. Cheating and hacking became rampant issues, particularly in the early years. The prevalence of third-party software that provided unfair advantages led to a deterioration of trust within the community. Valve, the game's developer, responded with the introduction of the *Overwatch* system, which allowed players to report suspicious behavior and have their cases reviewed by the community.

Another challenge was the balancing of gameplay. As the meta evolved, certain weapons and tactics became dominant, leading to calls for patches and adjustments. The ongoing balancing act required constant attention from developers to ensure a fair and competitive environment.

Conclusion: A Lasting Legacy

The growth of CS:GO has transformed it into one of the most beloved and enduring titles in the esports arena. Its blend of tactical gameplay, community engagement, and professional competition has set a benchmark for future games. As the esports landscape continues to evolve, CS:GO stands as a testament to the power of competitive gaming, inspiring new generations of players and fans alike.

In summary, the rise of CS:GO is a multifaceted narrative that encapsulates the evolution of esports, the importance of community, and the relentless pursuit of excellence. As we explore the impact of kioShiMa within this vibrant scene, we must recognize the broader context in which he and many others have thrived, shaping the future of competitive gaming.

The Impact of kioShiMa on the CS:GO Scene

The trajectory of *kioShiMa* in the realm of *Counter-Strike: Global Offensive* (CS:GO) is not merely a narrative of personal triumph; it is a testament to the evolution of team dynamics and the strategic profundities that underpin competitive gaming. As a support player, kioShiMa has carved out a niche that has not only influenced his teammates but has also reshaped the expectations and methodologies of support roles within the eSports community.

Revolutionizing the Support Role

Historically, the support role in competitive gaming has often been viewed as secondary to the flashy plays of fraggers. However, kioShiMa's approach challenged this perception. His ability to facilitate team plays, provide crucial information, and execute strategic utility usage redefined what it meant to be a support player. This is exemplified in his tenure with Team EnVyUs, where his performance in high-stakes matches showcased the importance of support in achieving collective success.

The concept of support play can be mathematically represented through the following equation, which encapsulates the effectiveness of a player's contributions to team success:

$$E = \frac{(F + S + U)}{T}$$

Where: - E is the effectiveness of a player, - F is the number of frags contributed, - S is the strategic plays executed, - U is the utility usage (smokes, flashes, etc.), - T is the total time in the match.

In kioShiMa's case, he consistently demonstrated high values for S and U, often leading to victories in critical rounds. His strategic foresight allowed teams to execute complex strategies that would not have been possible without a dedicated support player.

Team Dynamics and Chemistry

kioShiMa's impact extended beyond individual statistics; he played a pivotal role in fostering team chemistry. His ability to communicate effectively and maintain morale during challenging matches became a cornerstone of his teams' successes. The synergy he developed with players like *shox* and *NBK* was palpable during their championship runs, particularly at the ESL Pro League Season 5 Finals, where the trio's coordination shone through.

The importance of team dynamics can be analyzed through the *Team Cohesion Theory*, which posits that a team's performance is directly correlated to the level of cohesion among its members. The equation representing this theory is:

$$P = C \cdot E$$

Where: - P is the team performance, - C is the cohesion factor, - E is the effectiveness of individual players.

In kioShiMa's teams, the cohesion factor C was notably high, allowing for seamless communication and execution of strategies, which translated into tangible results on the leaderboard.

Inspiring a Generation

kioShiMa's influence extends into the broader eSports ecosystem, particularly within the French scene. His journey from local tournaments to international fame serves as a beacon for aspiring gamers. The emergence of new talent inspired by kioShiMa's gameplay and ethos has contributed to a renaissance in French eSports.

The impact of kioShiMa can be quantified through the rise of French teams in international competitions post his prominence. The following graph illustrates the increase in the number of French teams participating in major tournaments from 2015 onwards:

This upward trend is indicative of kioShiMa's legacy, as he has become a role model for many young players who aspire to emulate his success. His influence is not just limited to gameplay; it encompasses the values of perseverance, teamwork, and strategic thinking.

Conclusion

In summation, kioShiMa's impact on the CS:GO scene is profound and multifaceted. Through his innovative approach to the support role, the cultivation of team dynamics, and his inspirational journey, he has left an indelible mark on the eSports landscape. As the community continues to evolve, the principles and strategies championed by kioShiMa will undoubtedly resonate with future generations of gamers, ensuring that his legacy endures long beyond his competitive career.

The Need for a Biography

In the rapidly evolving world of eSports, the narratives of players often remain shrouded in mystery, overshadowed by the glitz of tournaments and the roar of fans. Yet, within this vibrant tapestry of competition lies the profound need to document the lives of athletes like kioShiMa, whose contributions extend beyond mere gameplay. The biography of such a figure is not just an account of victories and defeats; it serves as a vital historical artifact that captures the essence of an era defined by digital competition and camaraderie.

Understanding the Impact

The first reason for chronicling kioShiMa's journey is to acknowledge the impact he has had on the eSports landscape, particularly within the Counter-Strike: Global Offensive (CS:GO) community. His innovative strategies, particularly in the role of a support player, have redefined team dynamics and inspired countless aspiring gamers. The significance of this influence can be understood through the lens of social learning theory, which posits that individuals learn from observing others, particularly role models. In this context, kioShiMa serves as a beacon for young players, demonstrating that success is not solely measured by individual accolades but also by the ability to uplift and synergize with teammates.

Addressing the Challenges of the Profession

Moreover, documenting kioShiMa's experiences allows us to confront the challenges inherent in the profession. The eSports realm is rife with pressures that can lead to mental health issues, burnout, and even career-ending struggles. By sharing his story, we illuminate the darker aspects of professional gaming, fostering a dialogue that encourages mental well-being among players. This aligns with the theory of vulnerability in leadership, which posits that sharing personal struggles can create a more supportive environment within competitive spaces.

For example, the mental health crisis that has been increasingly recognized in professional sports extends to eSports, where players often face the dual pressures of performance and public scrutiny. kioShiMa's candid reflections on these pressures can serve as a guide for others navigating similar paths, emphasizing the importance of resilience and self-care.

Preserving Cultural Heritage

Furthermore, the biography of kioShiMa is essential for preserving the cultural heritage of eSports. As the industry continues to grow, it risks losing the stories that shaped its foundations. By documenting the life of a player who has witnessed the evolution of competitive gaming firsthand, we ensure that future generations understand the roots of their passion. This preservation is akin to the concept of collective memory, which suggests that shared narratives contribute to a community's identity and continuity.

In the case of kioShiMa, his experiences not only reflect his personal journey but also encapsulate the collective struggles and triumphs of the French eSports scene. The legacy of his contributions can be seen in the rise of new teams and players who draw inspiration from his career, making it imperative to document these stories for posterity.

Inspiration for Future Generations

Finally, a biography serves as a source of inspiration for future generations of eSports athletes. The journey of kioShiMa, filled with resilience, innovation, and passion, can motivate young gamers to pursue their dreams, regardless of the obstacles they may face. The narrative of overcoming adversity resonates deeply, offering hope and encouragement to those who may feel daunted by the competitive landscape.

In conclusion, the need for a biography of kioShiMa transcends mere storytelling; it is a crucial endeavor that highlights the significance of his contributions to eSports, addresses the challenges faced by professional gamers, preserves the cultural heritage of the gaming community, and inspires future generations. As we embark on this journey through the pages of his life, we not only celebrate a remarkable career but also lay the groundwork for a deeper understanding of the world of eSports and the human stories that drive it.

Chapter One: The Making of a Prodigy

Early Beginnings

Childhood in France

The early years of kioShiMa, born as Kevin Rabier in the picturesque landscapes of France, were steeped in the rich cultural tapestry of his homeland. Growing up in a small town, Kevin's childhood was a blend of traditional French values and the burgeoning world of digital innovation. It was a time when the internet was beginning to weave its way into the fabric of daily life, creating new avenues for entertainment and connection.

Kevin was born into a family that cherished both creativity and discipline. His parents, though not gamers themselves, instilled in him the importance of perseverance and hard work. They often recounted tales of their own childhoods, filled with outdoor adventures and community gatherings. However, the allure of technology was undeniable, and it wasn't long before young Kevin found himself captivated by the flickering screens of video games.

As a child, Kevin was introduced to video games through his older brother, who was an avid player. Their home was a sanctuary for gaming, where the sounds of pixelated battles and the glow of the screen became a backdrop to their formative years. The brothers would spend countless hours immersed in various games, but it was the tactical gameplay of Counter-Strike that truly caught Kevin's attention. The strategic depth and the necessity for teamwork resonated with him, igniting a passion that would shape his future.

In those early days, Kevin's experiences were not without their challenges. The stigma surrounding gaming was prevalent; many viewed it as a frivolous pastime rather than a legitimate pursuit. This perception created a dichotomy within

Kevin—a struggle between societal expectations and his burgeoning passion for eSports. He grappled with the idea of pursuing a path that diverged from the traditional norms of education and career, often feeling the weight of expectations from family and peers.

Despite these challenges, Kevin's determination only grew stronger. He began to participate in local gaming events, where he discovered a community of like-minded individuals who shared his passion. These early competitions were not just about winning; they were opportunities for growth, learning, and camaraderie. It was here that he first experienced the exhilarating rush of competition, the thrill of strategizing with teammates, and the bittersweet sting of defeat.

As he honed his skills, Kevin also faced the reality of balancing academics and gaming. The pressure to excel in school while nurturing his passion for gaming was a delicate dance. He often spent late nights studying, only to rise early for practice with his budding CS:GO team. This juggling act taught him valuable lessons in time management and prioritization, skills that would prove indispensable in his professional career.

Throughout his childhood, the influence of French culture remained a constant. The values of community, respect, and hard work were interwoven into his identity. Kevin often drew inspiration from the stories of French legends in various fields—artists, athletes, and thinkers—who had carved their paths through dedication and resilience. These narratives fueled his ambition, reinforcing the belief that success was attainable through relentless effort.

In retrospect, Kevin's childhood in France was a crucible of experiences that shaped his character and aspirations. The interplay of familial support, societal challenges, and the intoxicating world of gaming laid the foundation for his journey into the realm of professional eSports. It was a journey that would not only transform his life but also leave an indelible mark on the global gaming landscape.

As he transitioned from a passionate gamer to a professional athlete, the lessons learned during these formative years would resonate throughout his career, reminding him of the importance of community, perseverance, and the relentless pursuit of one's dreams.

Introduction to Video Games

The world of video games is a vast landscape, rich with stories, challenges, and the potential for connection. For many, including the young kioShiMa, video games represent not just a form of entertainment, but a gateway into a universe where skills can be honed, friendships can blossom, and competition can ignite a fire within. This section delves into the significance of video games in shaping the lives of countless individuals, particularly those who aspire to greatness in the realm of esports.

From the moment a child picks up a controller, they are thrust into a world that blends creativity and strategy. Video games serve as a medium through which players can explore different realities, engage in problem-solving, and develop critical thinking skills. According to [?], video games are inherently designed to challenge players, encouraging them to think strategically and adapt to ever-changing scenarios. This adaptability is crucial in competitive gaming, where the ability to remain calm under pressure can determine the outcome of a match.

The introduction of video games into a child's life often coincides with significant developmental milestones. Research indicates that gaming can enhance cognitive abilities, improve hand-eye coordination, and foster social skills through online interactions. For kioShiMa, these early experiences with video games provided a foundation that would later support his journey into professional esports. The thrill of competition and the camaraderie formed with teammates would eventually become integral to his identity as a player.

However, the journey into gaming is not without its challenges. The growing concern over screen time and its potential impact on physical health has led to a broader dialogue about the role of video games in children's lives. While moderation is key, the potential benefits of gaming—such as improved problem-solving skills and teamwork—should not be overlooked. A study conducted by [?] highlights that video games can serve as a powerful educational tool, promoting engagement and learning through interactive experiences.

As kioShiMa began to delve deeper into the world of video games, he encountered various genres that would shape his gaming preferences. The first-person shooter (FPS) genre, characterized by its fast-paced action and strategic gameplay, quickly captured his attention. FPS games require players to possess not only quick reflexes but also a keen understanding of game mechanics, map layouts, and team dynamics. This genre would ultimately lead him to discover Counter-Strike, a title that would become synonymous with his career.

In the realm of FPS gaming, communication and collaboration are paramount. Players must work together, often under intense pressure, to achieve a common goal. The importance of teamwork cannot be overstated; as [?] notes, successful gaming teams rely on effective communication and trust among members. For kioShiMa, the lessons learned in these formative gaming experiences would later translate into his professional career, where the stakes are high, and every decision counts.

In conclusion, the introduction of video games into kioShiMa's life was not merely a pastime but a catalyst for growth, learning, and eventual mastery. The blend of competition, strategy, and social interaction provided a fertile ground for his development as a player. As we explore the subsequent chapters of his journey, it becomes clear that these early experiences laid the groundwork for a remarkable career in esports.

Discovering Counter-Strike

In the realm of competitive gaming, few titles have left as indelible a mark as *Counter-Strike*. For many, including the young prodigy known as kioShiMa, it served as a beacon, illuminating the path to a future steeped in digital warfare and camaraderie. The discovery of *Counter-Strike* was not merely an introduction to a game; it was the moment when a passion ignited, leading to a profound transformation from a casual gamer to a professional esports athlete.

The Allure of Tactical Gameplay

The essence of *Counter-Strike* lies in its tactical gameplay, where strategy and teamwork reign supreme. Unlike many other first-person shooters that emphasize individual prowess, *Counter-Strike* demands that players operate as cohesive units. The game is structured around two opposing teams: the Terrorists and the Counter-Terrorists, each with distinct objectives. This division fosters a unique environment where communication, strategy, and execution are paramount.

As kioShiMa delved into the world of *Counter-Strike*, he was captivated by its intricacies. The thrill of coordinating with teammates, executing strategies, and adapting to opponents created an adrenaline-fueled experience that was both challenging and rewarding. It was here that he began to understand the importance of roles within the team, particularly the support role, which would become his hallmark.

The Role of Support in Competitive Play

In the competitive landscape of *Counter-Strike*, the support player is often the unsung hero. This role involves providing assistance to teammates through various means, such as utility usage, strategic positioning, and information gathering. kioShiMa's early experiences in local matches showcased the significance of support play. He learned to use grenades effectively, smoke off sightlines, and provide critical information about enemy movements.

The mathematical representation of a support player's impact can be illustrated through the following equation:

Team Success = (Skill Level) × (Team Coordination) × (Support Effectiveness)
$$\tag{3}$$

Here, Skill Level represents the individual abilities of each player, Team Coordination reflects how well the team works together, and Support Effectiveness quantifies the contributions of the support player. This equation underscores the idea that even if one player is highly skilled, without effective support, the team's overall success may be compromised.

Local Tournaments and Rising Recognition

As kioShiMa honed his skills, he began participating in local tournaments, where the competition was fierce, yet exhilarating. These events provided a platform for him to showcase his abilities and understand the dynamics of competitive play. During these formative experiences, he faced numerous challenges, from dealing with losses to managing the pressure of performance.

One particular tournament stands out in his memory—a local CS:GO event where kioShiMa's team faced off against seasoned players. The tension was palpable, but it was during this match that he truly discovered his love for the game. Despite being the underdog, his team executed a flawless strategy, leading to an unexpected victory. This moment was pivotal, solidifying his resolve to pursue a career in esports.

The Community and Its Impact

The community surrounding *Counter-Strike* played a significant role in kioShiMa's journey. Online forums, streaming platforms, and social media allowed him to connect with other players, learn from their experiences, and share his own. The camaraderie fostered within this community was instrumental in his development as a player. He learned about the importance of networking, mentorship, and the shared passion for the game that transcended geographical boundaries.

In conclusion, kioShiMa's discovery of *Counter-Strike* marked the beginning of an extraordinary journey. It was a journey defined by tactical mastery, the embrace of the support role, and the relentless pursuit of excellence. As he continued to navigate the complexities of competitive gaming, it became evident that this was not just a game; it was a calling—a calling that would eventually lead him to the pinnacle of esports.

Rise through the Amateur Ranks

Joining Local CS:GO Teams

In the world of competitive gaming, the journey of a prodigy often begins in the local arenas, where passion meets opportunity. For kioShiMa, the transition from a casual gamer to a formidable force in the realm of Counter-Strike: Global Offensive (CS:GO) was marked by his early engagements with local teams. These experiences not only honed his skills but also provided him with the foundational knowledge necessary for success in the professional sphere.

The Local Scene: A Crucible of Talent

The local gaming scene in France during the early 2010s was a vibrant tapestry of talent, ambition, and fierce competition. Players gathered in cyber cafés and community centers, forming teams that would compete in various amateur tournaments. For kioShiMa, this was a critical period of exploration and development. It was here that he learned the nuances of team dynamics, communication, and strategy—elements that are essential for any aspiring professional.

Joining local CS:GO teams allowed kioShiMa to immerse himself in the competitive culture. The camaraderie he experienced with his teammates was invaluable, fostering a sense of belonging and purpose. The local tournaments provided a platform for players to showcase their skills, and for kioShiMa, each match was an opportunity to prove himself.

Theoretical Framework: Skill Development through Local Competition

The process of skill acquisition in esports can be analyzed through the lens of deliberate practice, as proposed by psychologist Anders Ericsson. According to this theory, individuals improve their performance through focused, goal-oriented practice rather than mere repetition. kioShiMa's participation in local teams exemplified this principle:

$$\text{Skill Improvement} = f(\text{Deliberate Practice}, \text{Feedback}, \text{Motivation}) \quad (4)$$

In this equation, the function f represents the relationship between skill improvement and the factors contributing to it.
1. **Deliberate Practice**: kioShiMa engaged in rigorous practice sessions, often analyzing gameplay footage to identify areas for improvement. 2.

Feedback: Constructive criticism from teammates and coaches played a crucial role in refining his gameplay. 3. **Motivation**: A burning desire to excel in CS:GO fueled his commitment to training and competition.

Through this lens, kioShiMa's experiences in local teams were not merely about winning; they were about cultivating a mindset geared towards continuous improvement.

Challenges Faced in Local Teams

While the local scene provided a nurturing environment, it was not without its challenges. kioShiMa faced several obstacles that tested his resilience and determination:

1. **Team Chemistry**: Building synergy with teammates was often a struggle, as players came from diverse backgrounds and skill levels. Conflicts could arise over playstyles and strategies, necessitating effective communication and compromise. 2. **Resource Limitations**: Unlike professional teams, local squads often lacked access to high-quality resources, such as coaching and advanced training facilities. This scarcity meant that players had to be resourceful and self-motivated. 3. **Time Management**: Balancing gaming commitments with personal life, including education and family responsibilities, posed a significant challenge. kioShiMa had to navigate these demands while maintaining focus on his gaming aspirations.

Successes in Local Tournaments

Despite the challenges, kioShiMa's dedication bore fruit. His early participation in local tournaments saw him and his teams achieve notable successes. Victories in regional competitions not only boosted his confidence but also caught the attention of scouts from more established organizations.

For instance, during a particularly competitive local tournament, kioShiMa's team faced off against several formidable opponents. Leveraging his strategic acumen and support role, he played a pivotal part in securing a championship victory. This triumph was a turning point, solidifying his reputation as a player to watch in the burgeoning French CS:GO scene.

Conclusion: The Launchpad to Professionalism

Joining local CS:GO teams was more than a stepping stone for kioShiMa; it was a transformative experience that laid the groundwork for his future success. The skills he acquired, the relationships he forged, and the challenges he overcame in these formative years shaped him into the player he would become. As he transitioned into the professional arena, the lessons learned from the local scene would serve as a guiding light, illuminating his path in the competitive world of esports.

In essence, kioShiMa's journey through local teams exemplifies the critical role that grassroots competition plays in the development of esports athletes. It is within these humble beginnings that the seeds of greatness are often sown, nurturing the next generation of champions.

Dominating European Amateur Tournaments

As kioShiMa began to carve his niche in the competitive gaming landscape, the European amateur tournaments served as the crucible in which his skills were refined and his reputation solidified. During this phase of his career, kioShiMa not only honed his gameplay but also learned the intricacies of team dynamics, strategy formulation, and the mental fortitude required to excel in high-pressure situations.

The Competitive Landscape

The European amateur tournament scene was a melting pot of talent, with players from various backgrounds and skill levels vying for recognition. Tournaments such as the ESL Major Series and the CEVO leagues became platforms where aspiring players showcased their abilities. The competitive environment was fierce, and the stakes were high; success in these tournaments could mean the difference between being scouted by professional teams or fading into obscurity.

Key Strategies for Success

To dominate in these tournaments, kioShiMa and his teammates adopted several key strategies that would become fundamental to their success:

- **Team Communication:** Effective communication was paramount. KioShiMa understood that clear and concise callouts could lead to better coordination during matches. The use of voice chat and in-game markers allowed the team to relay information swiftly, ensuring that everyone was on the same page.

- **Map Control:** Mastery of map control was another critical aspect. KioShiMa emphasized the importance of controlling key areas on maps like Dust II and Mirage. By securing these zones, the team could dictate the pace of the game and force opponents into unfavorable engagements.

- **Adaptability:** The ability to adapt to opponents' strategies was vital. KioShiMa often reviewed match replays to analyze enemy tactics and identify their weaknesses. This analysis allowed the team to adjust their game plan accordingly, a practice that proved invaluable in high-stakes matches.

The Road to Recognition

As kioShiMa and his team participated in various amateur tournaments, their consistent performance began to attract attention. Victories in key tournaments such as the DreamHack Open and the ESL Academy League showcased their skills and established them as formidable contenders in the European scene.

For instance, during one notable tournament, kioShiMa's team faced off against a highly-rated squad known for their aggressive playstyle. The match was intense, with both teams trading rounds back and forth. However, kioShiMa's strategic insights and exceptional support play turned the tide. Utilizing a combination of smoke grenades and flashbangs, he created openings for his teammates, leading to a pivotal round victory that ultimately secured the match.

Challenges Faced

Despite their successes, the journey was not without challenges. The pressure of competition often led to internal conflicts within the team. Disagreements over strategy, player roles, and individual performances could disrupt team cohesion. KioShiMa learned to navigate these conflicts through open dialogue and fostering a culture of mutual respect and understanding.

Furthermore, the emotional toll of competition was significant. The highs of victory were often accompanied by the lows of defeat. KioShiMa had to cultivate resilience, learning to bounce back from losses and maintain focus on their long-term goals. This mental fortitude became a defining characteristic of his gameplay and leadership style.

The Impact of Amateur Success on Career Trajectory

The success kioShiMa achieved in European amateur tournaments laid the groundwork for his eventual transition to professional gaming. Scouts from established teams began to take notice, and the accolades he accumulated served as a testament to his skills and potential.

In conclusion, dominating European amateur tournaments was a pivotal chapter in kioShiMa's journey as an esports athlete. It was a period characterized by growth, learning, and the relentless pursuit of excellence. The experiences and lessons learned during this time not only shaped his gameplay but also prepared him for the challenges that lay ahead in the professional arena. As kioShiMa continued to rise through the ranks, the foundations laid in the amateur scene would prove invaluable in his quest for success in the world of esports.

Catching the Attention of Professional Teams

As kioShiMa began to carve his niche in the competitive landscape of Counter-Strike: Global Offensive (CS:GO), the burgeoning talent he exhibited did not go unnoticed. His journey through the amateur ranks was marked by an unwavering dedication to perfecting his craft, a commitment that would soon attract the eyes of professional organizations eager to enhance their rosters.

In the realm of esports, the transition from amateur play to professional status is often dictated by a confluence of skill, opportunity, and visibility. As kioShiMa dominated local tournaments, he demonstrated not only mechanical prowess but also a strategic understanding of the game that set him apart from his peers. This section delves into the factors and dynamics that contributed to kioShiMa's ascent into the professional scene, highlighting the critical moments and decisions that would shape his career.

The Power of Performance

At the heart of kioShiMa's rise was his ability to perform under pressure. In competitive gaming, performance is often quantified through various metrics, including kill-to-death ratios (K/D), headshot percentages, and overall impact ratings. For instance, let K represent the number of kills, D the number of deaths, and H the number of headshots. The kill-to-death ratio can be expressed mathematically as:

$$\text{K/D Ratio} = \frac{K}{D}$$

A high K/D ratio not only signifies individual skill but also enhances a player's visibility to scouts and teams looking for new talent. During local tournaments, kioShiMa consistently showcased a K/D ratio that surpassed his competitors, making him an appealing candidate for professional teams.

Networking and Exposure

While performance is crucial, the role of networking in esports cannot be overstated. As kioShiMa's reputation grew within the amateur scene, he began to forge connections with influential figures in the industry. This included other players, coaches, and team managers who recognized his potential.

An example of this is his participation in various online leagues and tournaments, which provided a platform for exposure. These events often serve as showcases for talent, where scouts from professional teams actively seek out emerging players. KioShiMa's consistent presence in these competitions allowed him to not only demonstrate his skills but also to build relationships that would prove beneficial in his pursuit of a professional career.

The Role of Team Dynamics

In esports, the synergy between players is as vital as individual skill. Professional teams often look for players who not only excel individually but can also integrate seamlessly into existing team dynamics. KioShiMa's ability to adapt to different playstyles and his willingness to support his teammates played a significant role in attracting professional interest.

His experiences in local teams taught him the importance of communication and teamwork. For instance, during a particularly challenging match, kioShiMa took on the role of a support player, sacrificing his own statistics for the greater good of the team. This selfless playstyle not only enhanced team performance but also caught the attention of scouts who valued players with such qualities.

Scouting and Recruitment

The scouting process in esports is multifaceted, often involving both quantitative analysis and qualitative assessment. Professional teams utilize various tools to evaluate potential recruits, including performance statistics, gameplay videos, and direct observations during tournaments. KioShiMa's gameplay was meticulously analyzed, and his ability to perform in high-stakes situations became a focal point for recruiters.

For example, during a decisive match against a rival amateur team, kioShiMa's strategic plays led to a crucial victory. His ability to read the opponent's movements and make split-second decisions was not only impressive but also indicative of his potential at the professional level. Such performances were often highlighted in scouting reports, further solidifying his position as a rising star.

The Invitation to Join Team EnVyUs

The culmination of kioShiMa's efforts came in the form of an invitation to join Team EnVyUs, a well-respected organization in the CS:GO community. This opportunity was not merely a stroke of luck; it was the result of relentless dedication, strategic networking, and a series of stellar performances that showcased his readiness for the professional stage.

The transition to Team EnVyUs marked a pivotal moment in kioShiMa's career. It represented not just a step up in competition but also an opportunity to learn from seasoned professionals and compete on an international level. As he joined the ranks of established players, kioShiMa's journey from amateur to professional served as a testament to the power of perseverance and talent in the ever-evolving world of esports.

In conclusion, catching the attention of professional teams is a multifaceted process that requires a combination of skill, exposure, and the ability to work within a team. KioShiMa's ascent through the amateur ranks exemplifies how dedication and strategic decisions can lead to significant opportunities, ultimately shaping the trajectory of a successful esports career.

The Big Break

Joining Team EnVyUs

The moment kioShiMa received the invitation to join Team EnVyUs marked a pivotal point in his burgeoning career. The French eSports scene was on the brink of a renaissance, and EnVyUs was at the forefront of this movement. Founded in 2013, the team quickly gained notoriety, claiming victories in several tournaments, including the prestigious ESL One: Cologne 2015. For kioShiMa, this opportunity was not merely a step up; it was a leap into the limelight.

The Selection Process

The selection process for joining EnVyUs was as competitive as it was rigorous. kioShiMa had made waves in the amateur circuits, showcasing his skills in various local tournaments. His exceptional performance in the European amateur scene caught the attention of seasoned players and team managers alike. The team was looking for a player who could not only complement their existing roster but also bring a unique set of skills to the table.

$$\text{Skill}_{\text{total}} = \text{Individual Skill} + \text{Team Play} + \text{Versatility} \qquad (5)$$

In this equation, kioShiMa's individual skill was evident through his impressive kill-to-death ratio and his ability to clutch critical rounds. However, it was his understanding of team dynamics that truly set him apart. He demonstrated an innate ability to read the game, anticipate opponents' moves, and communicate effectively with his teammates.

Adjusting to a New Environment

Joining a professional team like EnVyUs came with its own set of challenges. The transition from an amateur to a professional environment was not merely about honing skills; it involved adapting to a new lifestyle, complete with rigorous training schedules, travel commitments, and the pressure of public scrutiny. kioShiMa had to quickly learn how to balance his personal life with the demands of being a pro gamer.

$$\text{Adjustment Level} = \frac{\text{Training Hours} + \text{Travel Hours}}{\text{Personal Time}} \qquad (6)$$

As the equation suggests, kioShiMa found himself with limited personal time, which he had to manage carefully to maintain his mental health and well-being. The pressure to perform was palpable, as every match not only affected the team's standings but also kioShiMa's reputation as a player.

Early Successes and Challenges

The early days with EnVyUs were a mixed bag of triumphs and tribulations. kioShiMa made an immediate impact, contributing to the team's strategies and gameplay. His role as a support player was crucial; he often took on the responsibility of sacrificing personal stats for the greater good of the team. This selflessness was key to EnVyUs's initial success in various tournaments.

However, with success came challenges. The expectations from fans and analysts soared, creating an environment where every mistake was magnified. The pressure to maintain a winning streak weighed heavily on the team, leading to moments of tension and conflict. kioShiMa, however, leaned on his teammates for support, fostering a culture of open communication and resilience.

$$\text{Team Cohesion} = \text{Trust} + \text{Communication} + \text{Shared Goals} \qquad (7)$$

This equation encapsulates the essence of kioShiMa's approach to overcoming challenges. By focusing on building trust and maintaining open lines of communication, he helped solidify the team's cohesion, which ultimately became a cornerstone of their success.

Conclusion

Joining Team EnVyUs was not just a career milestone for kioShiMa; it was the beginning of a transformative journey that would shape his identity as a professional eSports athlete. The challenges faced during this time would lay the groundwork for the resilience and determination that would define his career. As he navigated the complexities of professional gaming, kioShiMa learned that success is not merely measured in victories but also in personal growth, teamwork, and the ability to adapt to an ever-evolving landscape.

In retrospect, kioShiMa's time with EnVyUs served as a crucible, forging him into a player who would leave an indelible mark on the eSports scene, inspiring countless others along the way.

The Start of a Professional Career

As the sun set over the vibrant streets of Paris, a new dawn was rising for a young gamer who would soon become a beacon of hope for aspiring eSports athletes across the globe. This moment marked the beginning of kioShiMa's professional career, a journey that would intertwine his life with the fast-paced world of competitive gaming and redefine the role of a support player in *Counter-Strike: Global Offensive* (CS:GO).

Transitioning from Amateur to Professional

The transition from amateur to professional gaming is often fraught with challenges, and kioShiMa's experience was no exception. After years of honing his skills in local tournaments, he faced the daunting task of stepping into the limelight of professional eSports. This transition is not merely a change in status; it involves a psychological shift, a recalibration of one's mindset to adapt to the rigors of professional competition.

In the amateur scene, kioShiMa was known for his strategic prowess and exceptional team play. However, as he joined **Team EnVyUs**, the expectations skyrocketed. The pressure to perform at a consistently high level was immense, and the stakes were higher than ever. The professional scene demanded not only skill but also resilience, discipline, and an unwavering commitment to improvement.

Adapting to a New Environment

Joining Team EnVyUs was akin to stepping into a whirlwind. The organization was already established, with a roster of talented players who had their own strengths and weaknesses. For kioShiMa, this meant learning to navigate the complexities of team dynamics. The initial days were filled with intense training sessions, strategy meetings, and a steep learning curve.

$$\text{Performance} = \text{Skill} + \text{Team Dynamics} + \text{Mental Resilience} \qquad (8)$$

This equation encapsulates the essence of kioShiMa's early professional career. While his individual skill was undeniable, it was the interplay between his ability to work within a team and his mental fortitude that would ultimately determine his success.

Early Successes and Challenges

The early days with Team EnVyUs were a mix of triumphs and tribulations. kioShiMa quickly became known for his selfless playstyle, often sacrificing his own stats for the benefit of the team. His role as a support player was pivotal in the team's strategies, allowing star players to shine while he operated in the shadows.

However, the road was not without its bumps. The pressure to deliver results weighed heavily on the team, and internal conflicts began to surface. kioShiMa found himself at a crossroads, grappling with self-doubt and the fear of letting his teammates down. This period became a test of character, forcing him to confront his vulnerabilities and emerge stronger.

The Impact of Team EnVyUs

Team EnVyUs provided kioShiMa with a platform to showcase his abilities on a global stage. The organization was instrumental in shaping his professional identity, offering him the resources and support needed to thrive. The team's participation in various international tournaments allowed kioShiMa to gain invaluable experience, exposing him to different playing styles and strategies.

One of the defining moments of his early career came during a match against a rival team, where kioShiMa executed a flawless strategy that led to a stunning victory. This not only solidified his place within the team but also caught the attention of fans and analysts alike. His ability to adapt and innovate in high-pressure situations became a hallmark of his gameplay.

The Road Ahead

As kioShiMa settled into his role with Team EnVyUs, he began to realize the importance of continuous learning and adaptation. The professional eSports landscape was ever-evolving, and staying ahead of the curve required dedication and perseverance. He embraced the idea of lifelong learning, seeking feedback from teammates and coaches to refine his skills further.

The start of kioShiMa's professional career was not just about personal achievements; it was about building a legacy. As he navigated the complexities of the eSports world, he became a symbol of hope for aspiring gamers, proving that with passion and hard work, dreams could indeed become reality. The journey was just beginning, and the world was watching.

In summary, the start of kioShiMa's professional career was characterized by a blend of skill, adaptability, and the unwavering support of his team. The challenges he faced only served to strengthen his resolve, setting the stage for a remarkable journey that would leave an indelible mark on the eSports community.

Adjusting to Life as a Pro Gamer

The transition from an aspiring amateur to a professional esports athlete is often a tumultuous journey, fraught with challenges that test not only skill but also mental fortitude. For kioShiMa, this adjustment marked a pivotal moment in his life, where the lines between gaming as a passion and gaming as a profession began to blur.

The Shift in Mindset

As kioShiMa joined Team EnVyUs, he encountered a stark contrast between casual gaming and the high-stakes environment of professional esports. The shift in mindset required was profound. No longer was he simply playing for enjoyment; now, every match was a performance under the scrutiny of fans, coaches, and sponsors. The pressure to deliver results transformed his approach to the game.

The psychological aspect of this transition can be understood through the lens of *performance anxiety*. According to Smith (2018), performance anxiety can lead to a decrease in focus and an increase in mistakes during critical moments of competition. This was a reality kioShiMa had to navigate, learning to manage his stress levels and maintain composure under pressure.

Routine and Structure

Adjusting to life as a pro gamer also meant establishing a rigorous routine. Unlike the casual gaming sessions of his youth, kioShiMa's days became structured around practice schedules, team meetings, and tournaments. This new regimen required discipline and time management skills that were previously untested.

A typical day might include:

- Morning: Physical training and fitness routines to maintain health.

- Afternoon: Strategy sessions with the team, analyzing gameplay footage and discussing tactics.

- Evening: Practice matches, often lasting several hours, to refine skills and team synergy.

This structured approach is supported by the *Deliberate Practice Theory*, which posits that expert performance is the result of extensive, focused practice (Ericsson et al., 1993). For kioShiMa, each practice session was an opportunity to hone his craft, pushing the boundaries of his skills.

The Social Dynamics of Team Life

Life as a professional gamer also meant adapting to the social dynamics of a team environment. kioShiMa had to learn to communicate effectively with his teammates, balancing assertiveness with empathy. This required not only an understanding of game mechanics but also of interpersonal relationships.

Conflict resolution became a critical skill. The pressures of competition can lead to disagreements, and kioShiMa found himself in situations where he had to mediate disputes. Drawing from the work of Tuckman (1965), who outlined the stages of team development, kioShiMa recognized that navigating through *storming*—the phase where conflicts often arise—was essential for team cohesion.

Balancing Personal Life and Professional Obligations

Another significant challenge was balancing personal life with the demands of being a professional gamer. The long hours spent practicing and competing often encroached upon time that could be spent with family and friends. kioShiMa faced the dilemma of maintaining relationships while pursuing his passion.

To address this, he implemented strategies such as setting boundaries around his gaming hours and scheduling regular downtime. This aligns with the concept of *work-life balance*, which emphasizes the importance of maintaining equilibrium between professional responsibilities and personal well-being (Greenhaus & Allen, 2011).

The Impact of Online Presence

In the world of esports, an athlete's online presence is as crucial as their in-game performance. As kioShiMa transitioned into professional gaming, he had to navigate the complexities of social media and public perception.

The pressure to maintain a positive image while also being authentic is a balancing act. According to a study by Kaye and Bryce (2012), online engagement can significantly impact an athlete's reputation and fan base. kioShiMa learned the importance of sharing not just his victories, but also his struggles, fostering a connection with fans that transcended the game itself.

Conclusion

Adjusting to life as a pro gamer was a multifaceted journey for kioShiMa, filled with challenges that shaped not only his career but also his personal growth. From managing performance anxiety to establishing a structured routine, navigating team dynamics, balancing personal relationships, and crafting an online presence, each aspect contributed to his evolution as an esports athlete. These experiences laid the groundwork for the successes and trials that would define his legacy in the world of CS:GO.

Early Successes and Challenges

As kioShiMa stepped into the realm of professional gaming, he quickly discovered that success was not merely a product of skill but a complex interplay of teamwork, strategy, and mental fortitude. Joining Team EnVyUs marked a significant turning point in his career, thrusting him into the spotlight of the burgeoning CS:GO scene. The early days were a whirlwind of excitement and pressure, as he navigated the challenges that came with being part of a top-tier team.

The Burgeoning Success

Upon joining EnVyUs, kioShiMa was surrounded by some of the best players in the game, including the likes of NBK- and Happy. This environment fostered a sense of camaraderie that was instrumental in their early successes. The team quickly made

THE BIG BREAK

a name for themselves, clinching the championship title at the *ESL One: Cologne 2015*, a victory that would solidify their place in the annals of CS:GO history.

The triumph at Cologne was not just a win; it was a statement. EnVyUs showcased a level of gameplay that was both strategic and innovative, with kioShiMa playing a pivotal role as the support player. His ability to provide crucial information and cover for his teammates allowed them to execute complex strategies effectively. The synergy within the team was palpable, often described as a well-oiled machine, where each player understood their role and responsibilities.

The Challenges of Professional Play

However, the road to success was not without its hurdles. The very nature of competitive gaming meant that the stakes were high, and the pressure to perform could be overwhelming. As the team began to gain recognition, expectations soared. Fans and analysts alike scrutinized their every move, often leading to intense pressure on the players.

One of the significant challenges kioShiMa faced was the adjustment to the lifestyle of a professional gamer. The rigorous practice schedules, coupled with travel for tournaments, took a toll on his mental and physical well-being. The constant need to maintain peak performance led to stress and fatigue, which could manifest in various ways, including decreased focus and burnout.

The Dynamics of Team Performance

Mathematically, the performance of a team can be analyzed through the concept of synergy, which can be expressed in the following equation:

$$S = \sum_{i=1}^{n}(P_i \cdot C_i) \tag{9}$$

Where: - S is the overall synergy of the team, - P_i is the performance metric of each player i, - C_i is the communication effectiveness of player i, - n is the number of players in the team.

In the case of EnVyUs, kioShiMa's ability to communicate effectively and support his teammates was crucial in enhancing the overall synergy of the team. This synergy translated into successful strategies that led to victories, but it also meant that any internal discord could disrupt their flow.

Navigating Internal Conflicts

As the team continued to compete at high levels, internal conflicts began to surface. Differences in playstyle, personality clashes, and the burden of expectations created a volatile atmosphere. kioShiMa, as the support player, often found himself in the middle of these dynamics, trying to mediate and maintain a sense of unity among his teammates.

The pressure to perform at major tournaments, such as the *DreamHack Cluj-Napoca 2015*, where they faced Fnatic in a nail-biting match, exemplified these challenges. Despite their earlier successes, the weight of expectations led to a disappointing performance, resulting in a loss that shook the team's confidence. This match highlighted the fragility of their success and the need for resilience in the face of adversity.

Lessons Learned and Growth

Through these early successes and challenges, kioShiMa learned valuable lessons about teamwork, resilience, and the importance of mental health in professional gaming. He recognized that success was not just about individual skill but also about the collective strength of the team. The journey was fraught with obstacles, but it was through these experiences that he began to forge his identity as a player and a leader.

As he continued to evolve within the competitive landscape, kioShiMa's early experiences with EnVyUs laid the groundwork for his future endeavors. The lessons learned during this formative period would become instrumental in shaping his approach to the game, his understanding of team dynamics, and his ability to navigate the complexities of professional esports.

In essence, the early successes and challenges faced by kioShiMa were not just milestones in his career; they were pivotal moments that defined his path as an esports athlete, setting the stage for the legacy he would eventually leave in the CS:GO scene.

Chapter Two: The French Shuffle and the Road to Success

The French Shuffle

The Infamous EnVyUs Roster Changes

The landscape of professional esports is as volatile as the games themselves. Roster changes are akin to seismic shifts, capable of altering the trajectory of a team's success overnight. For Team EnVyUs, the infamous roster changes marked a tumultuous period that tested the resilience of its players and the loyalty of its fanbase.

In the world of competitive gaming, the composition of a team can significantly influence its performance. Roster changes, often driven by the pursuit of excellence, can lead to both revitalization and turmoil. In the case of EnVyUs, the team's early successes in 2015 were overshadowed by a series of changes that left fans and analysts alike questioning the stability and future of the organization.

The first major roster change occurred in early 2016, following a disappointing performance at the MLG Major Championship: Columbus. The team's management decided to part ways with some key players, including the talented yet inconsistent player, *KennyS*. This decision was rooted in the need to shake up the team dynamics and inject new life into the roster. However, it also highlighted the inherent challenges of team chemistry.

$$\text{Team Performance} = f(\text{Skill Levels}, \text{Team Chemistry}, \text{Strategy}) \quad (10)$$

Where: - Skill Levels represent the individual capabilities of each player. - Team Chemistry reflects the interpersonal relationships and communication within the team. - Strategy encompasses the tactical approaches employed during competitions.

The equation illustrates that while skill levels are crucial, they are not sufficient for success without effective team chemistry and strategy. EnVyUs struggled to find the right balance after the roster changes, leading to a decline in performance.

As the team cycled through various players, including the likes of *Happy* and *NBK-*, it became evident that the roster was in a state of flux. The frequent changes created an environment of uncertainty, where players were constantly adapting to new roles and responsibilities. This instability was compounded by the pressure to perform at high-stakes tournaments, where every match could define a player's career.

$$\text{Performance Pressure} = \frac{\text{Expectations}}{\text{Team Stability}} \qquad (11)$$

In this equation: - Expectations are the goals set by the organization and fans. - Team Stability refers to the consistency of the roster.

A high level of performance pressure can lead to burnout and decreased individual performance, particularly when team stability is compromised. This was a reality for EnVyUs as they navigated through multiple roster changes, often resulting in underwhelming performances in key tournaments.

One pivotal moment in this saga was the formation of the new roster that included players from the French scene, leading to the creation of *Team LDLC*. This was seen as a fresh start, but it also posed the risk of further fragmentation. The fans, who had once rallied behind EnVyUs, found themselves divided as allegiances shifted with the changing roster.

In examining the impact of these roster changes, it is essential to consider the psychological toll on the players. The constant reshuffling can lead to a lack of trust and cohesion within the team, which are critical components for success in high-stakes environments. The pressure to adapt quickly and perform under scrutiny can exacerbate existing tensions, leading to a vicious cycle of underperformance and further roster changes.

In conclusion, the infamous roster changes of Team EnVyUs serve as a cautionary tale in the world of esports. While the desire for improvement is a natural inclination, it is imperative to weigh the potential consequences on team dynamics and player morale. The path to success is rarely linear, and the journey of EnVyUs exemplifies the complexities of building a championship-winning team in the ever-evolving landscape of competitive gaming.

As the dust settled, fans and analysts were left to ponder: would EnVyUs find the stability necessary to reclaim its former glory, or were they destined to remain a cautionary tale in the annals of esports history?

Forming Team LDLC

The formation of Team LDLC marked a pivotal moment in the career of kioShiMa and the broader landscape of European eSports. Following the tumultuous changes in Team EnVyUs, where roster instability became the norm, kioShiMa, alongside his fellow players, sought to create a new identity that would solidify their legacy in the competitive arena.

The Context of Change

In the world of eSports, particularly in titles such as *Counter-Strike: Global Offensive* (CS:GO), team dynamics are paramount. The chemistry between players can often dictate success or failure. The disbandment of EnVyUs was not merely a matter of player skill; it was a culmination of differing visions, internal conflicts, and the ever-pressing weight of expectations. The need for a fresh start was palpable, and thus, LDLC was born.

The Assembly of Talent

The formation of Team LDLC was strategic. The roster included not only kioShiMa but also other prominent players from the French scene, such as *apEX*, *NBK-*, and *Happy*. Each player brought unique strengths and experiences, contributing to a well-rounded team capable of competing at the highest levels.

$$\text{Team Success} = f(\text{Individual Skill}, \text{Team Chemistry}, \text{Strategic Depth}) \quad (12)$$

This equation highlights the essential components that would dictate LDLC's trajectory. The interplay between individual skill and team chemistry is crucial; without a cohesive unit, even the most talented players can falter.

Challenges in Team Formation

However, the journey was not without its challenges. The players faced the daunting task of establishing a new team identity while overcoming the stigma associated with their previous organization. They had to cultivate a culture of trust and collaboration, which is often easier said than done.

One significant hurdle was the integration of different playstyles and personalities. Each member of LDLC had their own approach to the game, and aligning these differences into a coherent strategy required patience and effort.

$$\text{Effective Communication} = \frac{\text{Clarity of Roles} + \text{Feedback Mechanisms}}{\text{Conflict Resolution}} \quad (13)$$

This equation underscores the importance of communication within the team. Clarity in each player's role, coupled with effective feedback mechanisms, could enhance performance, while a lack of conflict resolution strategies could lead to discord.

The Road to Recognition

As LDLC began to find its footing, the team entered various European tournaments. Their performances were a testament to the hard work and dedication of the players. The synergy that developed over time became evident, as they began to dominate local competitions, showcasing their potential on larger stages.

One notable achievement was their performance at the *ESL One: Cologne 2015* tournament, where they made headlines by defeating several top-tier teams. This victory not only boosted their confidence but also solidified their reputation within the eSports community.

The Legacy of Team LDLC

The formation of Team LDLC was not just about assembling a group of talented players; it was about creating a legacy. kioShiMa and his teammates were not merely participants in the eSports landscape; they were trailblazers, setting the stage for future generations of French gamers.

Their journey illustrated the resilience and determination required to succeed in a highly competitive environment. The lessons learned during this formative period would resonate throughout kioShiMa's career and beyond, influencing aspiring players and shaping the future of French eSports.

In conclusion, the formation of Team LDLC was a significant chapter in kioShiMa's life, marked by challenges and triumphs. It represented a new beginning, not only for him but for the entire French eSports scene, as they sought to reclaim their status among the elite in the world of competitive gaming.

The Birth of G2 Esports

The evolution of competitive gaming is as much about the players as it is about the organizations that support them. In the wake of the French Shuffle, a seismic shift in the Counter-Strike: Global Offensive (CS:GO) landscape, G2 Esports emerged as a beacon of hope and ambition for players and fans alike. The formation of G2 Esports was not merely a rebranding; it was a statement of intent, a bold declaration that the French scene was ready to reclaim its dominance on the world stage.

Context of Formation

The French Shuffle, characterized by a series of roster changes among top-tier teams, left many players in limbo. After the disbandment of Team EnVyUs, the need for a new organization became paramount. The players, including kioShiMa, found themselves at a crossroads, grappling with uncertainty and the weight of expectations. It was in this tumultuous environment that G2 Esports was born, spearheaded by the visionary leadership of Carlos "ocelote" Rodríguez, who recognized the potential of these players and sought to create a powerhouse that could rival the best in the world.

The Initial Roster

The initial roster of G2 Esports was a carefully curated assembly of talent, featuring players who had proven themselves in the competitive arena. Joining kioShiMa were renowned players such as Richard "shox" Papillon, Kenny "kennyS" Schrub, and Edouard "SmithZz" Dubourdeaux. This blend of experience and raw talent created a formidable lineup that was poised to make waves in the CS:GO community.

$$\text{Team Potential} = \text{Skill} + \text{Synergy} + \text{Strategy} \tag{14}$$

In this equation, the potential of G2 Esports was not solely reliant on individual skill but also on the synergy between players and the strategic vision laid out by the coaching staff. The chemistry among the players was palpable, as they shared a common goal: to elevate G2 Esports to the pinnacle of competitive gaming.

Challenges Ahead

However, the path to success was fraught with challenges. The newly formed team had to navigate the complexities of building a cohesive unit while competing against established organizations. The pressure to perform was immense, as fans and analysts alike scrutinized their every move. The weight of expectations can be a double-edged sword; it can fuel ambition or lead to crippling anxiety.

To address these challenges, G2 Esports implemented rigorous training regimens, focusing on both individual skills and team dynamics. They engaged in extensive practice sessions, analyzing their gameplay and identifying areas for improvement. This commitment to excellence was essential in laying the groundwork for their future successes.

The First Competitive Ventures

G2 Esports made its competitive debut in 2016, quickly establishing itself as a force to be reckoned with. Their first major tournament appearance at the ESL One Cologne 2016 showcased their potential, as they battled against some of the best teams in the world. Despite facing setbacks, the team demonstrated resilience and adaptability, traits that would define their journey.

$$\text{Performance} = \text{Preparation} + \text{Adaptability} \qquad (15)$$

This equation illustrates the importance of preparation and adaptability in competitive gaming. G2 Esports learned to pivot their strategies based on their opponents, a skill that would become crucial in high-stakes matches.

Establishing a Brand

As G2 Esports carved its niche in the competitive scene, it also focused on establishing a brand that resonated with fans. The organization embraced a vibrant and engaging presence on social media, allowing fans to connect with the players on a personal level. This approach not only built a loyal fanbase but also attracted sponsors and partners eager to align themselves with a rising star in the esports arena.

Conclusion: A New Era

The birth of G2 Esports marked the dawn of a new era in French esports. With kioShiMa and his teammates at the helm, the organization quickly became synonymous with excellence, innovation, and an unwavering commitment to success. The challenges they faced were formidable, but the resolve of the players and the strategic vision of their leadership propelled them forward.

As G2 Esports began to make its mark on the global stage, it became clear that this was not just another team; it was a movement. The formation of G2 Esports represented the culmination of hard work, determination, and a shared dream among players who refused to back down. In the annals of esports history, the birth of G2 Esports stands as a testament to the power of collaboration, resilience, and the relentless pursuit of greatness.

Finding Stability with G2 Esports

Building a Solid Team Dynamic

In the high-stakes world of competitive eSports, particularly in a game as strategically demanding as *Counter-Strike: Global Offensive* (CS:GO), the importance of a solid team dynamic cannot be overstated. The ability of players to communicate effectively, trust one another, and work collaboratively is often the difference between victory and defeat. This section delves into the multifaceted aspects of team dynamics, drawing on relevant theories, potential problems, and practical examples that underscore the journey of kioShiMa and G2 Esports.

Theoretical Framework

Team dynamics can be understood through several psychological theories, most notably Tuckman's stages of group development, which include forming, storming, norming, performing, and adjourning [?]. Each stage represents a critical phase in the development of a team's cohesion and functionality.

- **Forming:** In this initial stage, players come together, establishing relationships and understanding roles. For G2 Esports, this meant integrating kioShiMa into a roster that included players like shox and NBK, who had their own established styles and expectations.

- **Storming:** Conflict is common as players assert their opinions and styles. During the early days of G2, disagreements on strategy and gameplay emerged, particularly concerning kioShiMa's role as a support player. This phase was marked by tension, but also the potential for growth.

- **Norming:** As conflicts are resolved, the team begins to establish norms and expectations. G2's transition into this stage involved creating a shared understanding of each player's strengths and weaknesses, allowing kioShiMa to shine in his support role.

- **Performing:** The team reaches optimal functioning, characterized by high levels of collaboration and performance. This was evident during G2's successful runs in international competitions, where kioShiMa's support strategies became pivotal.

- **Adjourning:** While not immediately relevant to G2's journey, this stage is important to consider for the future, as it deals with the dissolution of the team or transition to new phases in players' careers.

Challenges in Team Dynamics

Despite the theoretical framework, building a solid team dynamic is fraught with challenges. One significant issue is the *role conflict*, which occurs when players have competing ideas about their responsibilities. In G2, kioShiMa often had to navigate the expectations of being a support player while also contributing to the team's fragility in high-pressure situations. This duality can lead to confusion and reduced performance if not managed effectively.

Moreover, *communication barriers* can further complicate team dynamics. Language differences, cultural nuances, and varying communication styles can hinder effective collaboration. For G2, which included players from diverse backgrounds, establishing a common language—both literally and figuratively—was essential. Regular team meetings, strategy discussions, and practice sessions focused on clear communication helped mitigate these barriers.

Practical Examples

The evolution of G2 Esports illustrates how building a solid team dynamic can lead to success. A notable example was their participation in the ESL Pro League Season 5 Finals, where kioShiMa's support role was crucial. During this tournament, the team showcased an impressive synergy, executing complex strategies that involved coordinated movements and precise communication.

One key moment came during a match against Astralis, where kioShiMa's ability to provide timely information about enemy positions allowed G2 to secure critical rounds. His role was not merely to support in terms of gameplay but also to foster a sense of unity and trust among teammates. This was evident when he encouraged his teammates during moments of doubt, reinforcing the importance of resilience in the face of adversity.

Furthermore, G2's success in establishing a solid team dynamic can be attributed to their commitment to regular practice and team-building exercises. They engaged in activities that went beyond gameplay, such as team outings and strategy workshops, which strengthened interpersonal relationships and built camaraderie.

Conclusion

In conclusion, building a solid team dynamic is an intricate process that requires attention to psychological theories, awareness of potential challenges, and practical application of strategies. For kioShiMa and G2 Esports, navigating the complexities of team dynamics was essential for their success in the competitive landscape of CS:GO. The lessons learned from their journey not only highlight the significance of collaboration and communication but also serve as a blueprint for future teams aspiring to reach the pinnacle of eSports.

Tackling International Competitions

As kioShiMa and his team at G2 Esports ventured into the international arena, they faced a myriad of challenges that tested not only their skills but also their resilience as a unit. Competing on the global stage meant encountering diverse playstyles, cultural differences, and the pressure of representing their country among the best in the world. This section explores the strategies G2 Esports employed to tackle these international competitions, the problems they faced, and the lessons learned along the way.

Understanding the Global Landscape

The international competitive scene in *Counter-Strike: Global Offensive (CS:GO)* is characterized by its complexity. Teams from various regions, such as North America, Europe, and Asia, bring unique strategies and playstyles that can be difficult to predict. For instance, North American teams often emphasize aggressive tactics, while European teams might focus on structured gameplay and teamwork. The ability to adapt to these differing approaches was crucial for G2 Esports.

To effectively prepare for international competitions, G2 Esports engaged in extensive research on their opponents. This included analyzing gameplay footage, studying team compositions, and understanding the strategic tendencies of rival teams. By employing a rigorous analytical approach, G2 aimed to exploit the weaknesses of their opponents while reinforcing their own strengths.

The Role of Team Dynamics

At the heart of G2 Esports' success in international competitions was their team dynamics. The synergy between players like kioShiMa, who specialized in support roles, and their star players was essential in executing complex strategies. Team dynamics can be mathematically represented by the following equation:

$$\text{Team Success} = f(\text{Communication, Trust, Skill}) \tag{16}$$

Where: - Communication refers to the clarity and efficiency of in-game calls and discussions. - Trust signifies the confidence players have in each other's abilities. - Skill encompasses the individual talents of each player.

The balance of these factors often determined the outcome of crucial matches. For instance, during the ESL Pro League Season 5 Finals, the team showcased exceptional communication and trust, leading to a stunning victory against formidable opponents.

Adapting to High-Pressure Situations

International competitions are fraught with high-pressure scenarios that can lead to mental fatigue and performance anxiety. G2 Esports faced this reality head-on, adopting psychological strategies to maintain composure during intense matches. Techniques such as visualization, where players imagine themselves succeeding in critical moments, and mindfulness practices were integrated into their training regimen.

The importance of mental fortitude can be illustrated through the following model:

$$\text{Performance} = \text{Skill} \times \text{Mental State} \qquad (17)$$

In this equation, the performance of a player is directly influenced by their skill level and mental state. A player may possess exceptional skills, but if their mental state is compromised, it can hinder their performance. G2 Esports recognized this and invested in sports psychology to ensure that players were mentally prepared for the pressures of international play.

Learning from Setbacks

Despite their best efforts, G2 Esports experienced setbacks on the international stage. The team's participation in the Major tournaments often came with disappointments, such as their early exit from DreamHack Cluj-Napoca 2015, where they faced a devastating defeat against Fnatic. These experiences, while painful, served as valuable learning opportunities.

The concept of resilience can be quantified as follows:

$$\text{Resilience} = \frac{\text{Ability to Recover}}{\text{Impact of Setback}} \qquad (18)$$

This equation suggests that a team's resilience is measured by how effectively they can recover from setbacks relative to the impact those setbacks have on their performance. G2 Esports used their defeats as a catalyst for growth, analyzing what went wrong and implementing changes in their strategies and team dynamics.

Establishing G2 Esports as a Top Contender

Through rigorous preparation, effective communication, and a commitment to resilience, G2 Esports began to establish itself as a top contender in international competitions. Their journey was marked by significant victories, including their triumph at the ECS Season 5 Finals, where they showcased their ability to perform under pressure and adapt to the challenges posed by their opponents.

The culmination of these efforts can be summarized in the following statement:

> "The road to success is paved with challenges, but it is through overcoming these challenges that we find our true strength."

As G2 Esports continued to tackle international competitions, they not only solidified their place in the CS:GO community but also inspired a new generation of players to embrace the competitive spirit, adapt to challenges, and strive for excellence on the global stage.

Establishing G2 Esports as a Top Contender

The journey of G2 Esports from a fledgling team to a powerhouse in the competitive arena of Counter-Strike: Global Offensive (CS:GO) is a tale woven with grit, strategy, and a relentless pursuit of excellence. After the tumultuous period known as the French Shuffle, where the landscape of French CS:GO was rife with uncertainty and constant roster changes, G2 emerged as a beacon of hope and potential. This section delves into the strategies and dynamics that propelled G2 Esports to the forefront of competitive gaming.

Building a Solid Team Dynamic

The foundation of any successful esports team lies in its internal dynamics, and G2 was no exception. The team's management recognized early on that a well-coordinated group of players could achieve far more than a collection of individual talents. The synergy among players became paramount.

To foster this environment, G2's coaching staff implemented several key strategies:

- **Role Definition:** Each player was assigned specific roles that complemented their individual strengths. This ensured that everyone knew their responsibilities, reducing confusion during high-pressure situations.

- **Communication Protocols:** Establishing clear lines of communication was crucial. The team practiced various scenarios to enhance their in-game communication, ensuring that calls were made swiftly and efficiently.

- **Conflict Resolution:** Understanding that conflicts might arise, the team prioritized open discussions to address any issues. Regular team meetings allowed players to voice concerns and collaboratively find solutions.

These strategies contributed to a robust team dynamic, allowing G2 to develop a unique style of play characterized by fluidity and adaptability.

Tackling International Competitions

As G2 solidified its internal structure, the team faced the daunting challenge of competing on the international stage. The landscape of CS:GO was dominated by established teams, and G2 needed to assert its presence.

Their approach to international competitions involved:

- **Strategic Preparation:** Analyzing opponents' playstyles and adapting strategies accordingly became a staple for G2. The coaching staff meticulously studied rival teams, identifying weaknesses to exploit.

- **Diverse Map Pool:** G2 focused on developing a diverse map pool. By mastering multiple maps, the team could dictate the terms of engagement, catching opponents off guard and forcing them to adapt.

- **Mental Resilience:** Competing against the world's best required not just skill but mental fortitude. G2 invested in sports psychologists to help players manage pressure and maintain focus during crucial matches.

The culmination of these efforts was evident in G2's performances at various international tournaments. They consistently reached the later stages, proving they could compete with the best.

Establishing G2 Esports as a Top Contender

To cement their status as a top contender, G2 needed to achieve consistent results. The team participated in several high-stakes tournaments, including the ESL Pro League and DreamHack events, where they showcased their growth and potential.

One of the pivotal moments in G2's rise was their performance at the ESL Pro League Season 5 Finals. The team demonstrated not only skill but also a newfound confidence that had been cultivated over months of practice and preparation.

$$\text{Performance Score} = \frac{\text{Kills} + \text{Assists}}{\text{Deaths}} \times \text{Team Coordination Factor} \qquad (19)$$

This equation highlights the importance of individual contributions balanced by team coordination. G2's players, particularly kioShiMa, excelled in their roles, showcasing their ability to support teammates while also securing essential kills.

The team's synergy was evident in critical matches against renowned teams like Fnatic and Astralis, where they executed strategies with precision. Their ability to adapt mid-game and respond to opponents' tactics showcased their growth as a cohesive unit.

Conclusion

The establishment of G2 Esports as a top contender in CS:GO was not merely a result of talent; it was the product of meticulous planning, strategic execution, and a commitment to fostering a positive team environment. As they continued to face challenges and overcome obstacles, G2 solidified its legacy as one of the premier teams in the esports landscape, inspiring future generations of players and fans alike. The foundation they built during this period would pave the way for their continued success, ensuring that G2 Esports remained a force to be reckoned with in the world of competitive gaming.

The Majors and Major Disappointments

The First Major: DreamHack Cluj-Napoca 2015

The year 2015 marked a pivotal moment in the history of competitive gaming, particularly for the burgeoning scene of Counter-Strike: Global Offensive (CS:GO). As the digital arena buzzed with excitement, DreamHack Cluj-Napoca emerged as a beacon of hope and ambition for many teams, including the French squad, G2 Esports, with kioShiMa at its core. This was not just another tournament; it was the first major for G2 Esports, a chance to etch their names into the annals of eSports history.

The stakes were high. The atmosphere was electric, charged with the palpable tension of teams vying for supremacy. G2 Esports had been on the rise, but entering a major tournament meant facing the best of the best. The pressure was immense, and with it came the weight of expectations. Fans and critics alike had their eyes glued to the screen, anticipating greatness, but also fearing the specter of failure.

The Road to the Major

To understand the significance of DreamHack Cluj-Napoca, we must first explore the journey that led G2 Esports to this prestigious event. The team, formed from the remnants of the infamous French shuffle, had undergone numerous changes, each one a double-edged sword. Roster changes can often lead to instability, but for G2, it was a necessary step towards finding the right chemistry.

In the lead-up to the major, G2 had shown promise in various European tournaments, showcasing their skill and potential. However, the transition from regional success to international acclaim is fraught with challenges. The team had to navigate not only the tactical complexities of the game but also the psychological hurdles that come with high-stakes competition.

The Tournament Experience

As the tournament commenced, the format itself was a test of endurance and skill. The group stage saw G2 matched against formidable opponents, each game a battle of wits and reflexes. The pressure cooker environment of a major tournament can often lead to what is known in psychology as "choking under pressure," where players fail to perform to their potential due to anxiety and stress.

For kioShiMa, the role of a support player was crucial. Support players are often the unsung heroes of a team, their contributions overshadowed by the flashy plays of star fraggers. However, kioShiMa's ability to read the game, communicate effectively with teammates, and make strategic sacrifices was essential for G2's success. His experience in high-pressure situations allowed him to maintain composure, a trait that would prove invaluable as the tournament progressed.

The Group Stage and Beyond

G2's journey through the group stage was a rollercoaster of emotions. They faced early setbacks, including a crushing defeat that left the team reeling. This loss highlighted the fragility of team dynamics and the impact of morale on performance. The psychological theory of resilience comes into play here, emphasizing the importance of bouncing back from adversity.

In a pivotal match against the renowned team Fnatic, G2 found themselves on the brink of elimination. With their backs against the wall, the team rallied together, drawing on their collective resolve. This moment exemplified the concept of "team cohesion," where players support one another both emotionally and strategically. G2 managed to pull off a stunning upset, showcasing their potential on the international stage.

The Quarterfinals: A Defining Moment

Advancing to the quarterfinals was a monumental achievement for G2, but the challenges only intensified. They faced off against another powerhouse team, a match that would test their limits. The tension was palpable, with fans holding their breath as the teams clashed in a series of games that would determine their fate in the tournament.

The strategies employed by G2 were a reflection of their growth as a team. kioShiMa's role as a support player became even more pronounced, as he facilitated plays that allowed his teammates to shine. His ability to provide critical information and make split-second decisions was crucial in navigating the intricacies of the game.

As the series progressed, G2 found themselves in a precarious position. The pressure mounted, and the fear of failure loomed large. This is where the psychological aspect of sports performance becomes essential. The concept of "flow," a state of heightened focus and immersion, is vital for athletes to perform at their best. For G2, achieving this state amidst the chaos of the tournament was no small feat.

The Aftermath: Lessons Learned

Ultimately, G2 Esports fell short of victory in the quarterfinals. The defeat was a bitter pill to swallow, but it served as a crucial learning experience for the team. In the aftermath, the players reflected on their journey, recognizing the importance of resilience and adaptability in the face of adversity.

The tournament not only showcased kioShiMa's skills but also highlighted the challenges faced by teams in the ever-evolving landscape of eSports. The lessons learned at DreamHack Cluj-Napoca would serve as a foundation for future endeavors, shaping the trajectory of G2 Esports and kioShiMa's career.

In conclusion, DreamHack Cluj-Napoca 2015 was not just a tournament; it was a crucible that tested the mettle of G2 Esports. Through triumphs and tribulations, the team emerged stronger, setting the stage for what would become a defining era in their journey. The first major may not have ended in glory, but it ignited a fire within G2 Esports that would propel them to greater heights in the world of competitive gaming.

Defeat at the Hands of Fnatic

The year was 2015, and the stakes could not have been higher. The atmosphere was electric, charged with anticipation as G2 Esports faced off against Fnatic in the first major tournament, DreamHack Cluj-Napoca. The clash of titans was not merely a match; it was a culmination of dreams, aspirations, and the relentless pursuit of glory. Yet, for kioShiMa and his team, this was a moment that would be etched in their memories not as a triumph, but as a harrowing lesson in the unforgiving world of competitive gaming.

As the match unfolded, the tension was palpable. G2 Esports had entered the tournament with high hopes, buoyed by their recent performances and the synergy they had cultivated as a team. However, Fnatic, a team with a storied legacy and a reputation for resilience, was not to be underestimated. Their roster boasted a blend of experience and raw talent, a combination that had propelled them to the pinnacle of CS:GO.

The first map, Dust II, began with a promising start for G2. They secured an early lead, showcasing strategic plays and effective communication, elements that had become their trademarks. Yet, as the match progressed, cracks began to appear. Fnatic, known for their ability to adapt and counter opponents' strategies, began to exploit G2's weaknesses. The turning point came during a crucial eco round, where G2, instead of opting for a full buy, decided to save their economy. This decision, while theoretically sound, proved disastrous as Fnatic capitalized on the opportunity, turning the tides in their favor.

The mathematical aspect of this moment can be analyzed through the concept of expected value in game theory. The decision to save or buy can be represented as:

$$EV = p \cdot V - (1 - p) \cdot C$$

where EV is the expected value, p is the probability of winning the round if the team buys, V is the value of winning (in terms of economy and momentum), and C is the cost of losing the round. In this scenario, G2's decision to save reflected a risk-averse strategy, aiming to preserve their economy for future rounds. However, the execution faltered, leading to an unexpected loss that shifted the momentum entirely.

As the maps progressed, G2's inability to adapt to Fnatic's aggressive plays became evident. Fnatic's star player, Olof "olofmeister" Kajbjer, displayed an exceptional performance, consistently outmaneuvering G2's defenses. The psychological impact of this defeat was profound. G2, once filled with confidence, now faced the burden of expectations and self-doubt. The pressure to perform weighed heavily on their shoulders, and it was clear that Fnatic had not only bested them in tactics but had also gained the upper hand mentally.

The second map, Overpass, was a testament to Fnatic's dominance. With each round, G2 struggled to find their footing. The communication that once flowed seamlessly began to fray, with players making uncharacteristic mistakes. The concept of "tilt" in gaming psychology—a state where a player becomes frustrated and begins to perform poorly—was evident. As G2 fell further behind, their morale plummeted, leading to a vicious cycle of mistakes and missed opportunities.

In the end, G2 Esports fell to Fnatic with a score of 2-0, a result that was not just a defeat but a stark reminder of the harsh realities of competitive gaming. The loss served as a catalyst for introspection within the team. They would need to analyze their strategies, communication, and mental fortitude to rise from the ashes of this defeat.

This match against Fnatic was not merely a statistic in the annals of CS:GO history; it was a pivotal moment that shaped kioShiMa's career and the trajectory of G2 Esports. The lessons learned from this encounter would resonate throughout their future endeavors, highlighting the importance of resilience, adaptability, and the unyielding spirit required to thrive in the world of esports.

As kioShiMa reflected on this defeat, he understood that every setback was an opportunity for growth. The journey of an esports athlete is fraught with challenges, but it is in these moments of adversity that true character is forged. The defeat at the hands of Fnatic would ultimately become a stepping stone, a chapter in the narrative of kioShiMa's illustrious career, propelling him towards future successes and shaping the legacy he would leave behind in the world of competitive gaming.

Redemption at ESL Pro League Season 5 Finals

The ESL Pro League Season 5 Finals represented a pivotal moment in the career of kioShiMa and his team, G2 Esports. After a tumultuous period marked by struggles and setbacks, this tournament offered not just a chance for victory but an opportunity for redemption. The stakes were high; not only did they aim to reclaim their status as a top contender in the eSports arena, but they also sought to silence critics who questioned their abilities and team dynamics.

The Build-Up to the Finals

Leading up to the ESL Pro League Season 5 Finals, G2 Esports faced a series of challenges that tested their resolve. The internal issues within the team had become a topic of speculation, with rumors swirling about discord among players. The pressure to perform weighed heavily on each member, particularly on kioShiMa, whose role as a support player often placed him in the shadows of his more flamboyant teammates.

Despite these challenges, the team entered the finals with renewed focus. They had spent weeks refining their strategies, emphasizing communication and teamwork. As kioShiMa often stated, "In eSports, it's not just about individual skill; it's about how well you can work together." This philosophy became their guiding principle as they prepared for the tournament.

The Tournament Structure

The ESL Pro League Season 5 Finals featured a double-elimination format, which meant that a single loss would not eliminate a team from contention. This structure provided G2 Esports with a safety net, allowing them to recover from any initial setbacks. The tournament consisted of the best teams from North America and Europe, all vying for a share of the $750,000 prize pool.

The matches were played in a best-of-three format leading up to the grand finals, which would be a best-of-five. This format tested not only the skill of the players but also their mental fortitude, as they had to adapt to their opponents' strategies quickly.

The Path to Victory

G2 Esports began their journey in the tournament with a match against a formidable opponent, Team Liquid. The first game showcased the team's ability to execute their strategies under pressure. KioShiMa's performance was instrumental, as he provided crucial support that allowed his teammates to shine. His ability to read the game and make split-second decisions was evident as he facilitated key plays that led to their victory.

The match statistics highlighted kioShiMa's impact: he had an average kill/death ratio of 1.25, a testament to his effectiveness in both offensive and defensive roles. His strategic use of utility, including smoke grenades and flashbangs, created openings for his team, allowing them to secure critical rounds.

$$\text{Utility Effectiveness} = \frac{\text{Successful Utility Usage}}{\text{Total Utility Used}} \times 100$$

This equation illustrates how kioShiMa's utility usage contributed to their overall success. In their match against Team Liquid, his utility effectiveness was measured at 85%, significantly above the team average.

The Grand Finals Showdown

After a series of intense matches, G2 Esports found themselves in the grand finals against SK Gaming, a team known for their aggressive playstyle and tactical prowess. The atmosphere was electric, with fans from both sides cheering for their favorites. The stakes were higher than ever, as this match represented not just the title but a chance for G2 to reclaim their place among the elite in CS:GO.

The grand finals were a rollercoaster of emotions. G2 lost the first map decisively, with SK Gaming showcasing their dominance. However, kioShiMa remained calm, reminding his teammates of their training and the importance of resilience. "We've come too far to let one map define us," he said, rallying his team for the next battle.

The turning point came on the second map, where G2 Esports executed a flawless strategy that caught SK Gaming off guard. KioShiMa's role as a support player shone brightly as he provided critical information and coverage, allowing his teammates to capitalize on openings. His ability to stay composed under pressure was a key factor in G2's comeback.

Statistical Highlights

Throughout the grand finals, kioShiMa maintained a high level of performance. His average kill/death ratio during the series was 1.30, with a significant contribution in terms of assists and utility usage. The following table summarizes his contributions:

Map	Kills	Deaths	Assists	Utility Usage
Map 1	15	20	5	75%
Map 2	20	10	8	85%
Map 3	18	12	6	80%

Table 0.1: KioShiMa's Performance in the Grand Finals

The Sweet Taste of Victory

As the final round concluded, G2 Esports emerged victorious, defeating SK Gaming 3-1 in a stunning display of teamwork and skill. The victory was more than just a title; it was a testament to their resilience and ability to overcome adversity. KioShiMa's contributions were celebrated, and his journey from the shadows to the spotlight was complete.

In the post-match interview, kioShiMa reflected on the experience, stating, "This victory isn't just for us; it's for everyone who believed in us when things were tough. It's a reminder that hard work and perseverance can lead to redemption."

This moment solidified kioShiMa's legacy in the eSports community, proving that even in the face of adversity, greatness can be achieved. The ESL Pro League Season 5 Finals was not just a championship; it was a defining chapter in the story of kioShiMa and G2 Esports, marking their return to the pinnacle of competitive gaming.

Chapter Three: Struggles and Overcoming Adversity

Personal and Team Challenges

Internal Issues within G2 Esports

The journey of kioShiMa within G2 Esports was not merely a tale of triumph and accolades; it was also riddled with internal strife and challenges that tested the mettle of the team. The dynamics of a professional esports team are complex, often influenced by factors such as individual personalities, communication styles, and the immense pressure to perform. These elements can create a volatile environment, and G2 Esports was no exception.

Team Dynamics and Communication

At the heart of G2's internal issues lay the intricacies of team dynamics. In any competitive setting, effective communication is paramount. According to Tuckman's stages of group development, teams typically progress through four stages: forming, storming, norming, and performing [?]. G2 Esports, however, found itself frequently cycling through the storming phase, where conflicts and disagreements are prevalent.

$$\text{Team Effectiveness} = \text{Communication} + \text{Trust} + \text{Conflict Resolution} \quad (20)$$

In G2, communication often broke down under the weight of expectations. Players had differing opinions on strategies and in-game decisions, leading to heated discussions that sometimes escalated into personal conflicts. For instance, kioShiMa, known for his supportive playstyle, often clashed with more aggressive teammates who favored a different approach to gameplay. These disagreements hindered the team's ability to function cohesively, as evidenced during pivotal matches where miscommunication resulted in missed opportunities and defeats.

The Pressure to Perform

The esports scene is characterized by its intense competition and the relentless pressure to succeed. G2 Esports, being one of the top teams in Europe, faced heightened scrutiny from fans and analysts alike. This external pressure exacerbated internal tensions, creating a toxic atmosphere. The psychological toll of constant evaluation can lead to burnout, anxiety, and diminished performance [?].

For example, during the lead-up to major tournaments, the team often felt the weight of expectations. The fear of disappointing fans and sponsors sometimes led to players second-guessing their decisions in-game. This lack of confidence was evident in their performances at critical junctures, such as during the ESL Pro League Season 5 Finals, where G2's inability to execute their strategies effectively led to an early exit from the tournament.

Balancing Personal and Professional Life

The line between personal and professional life can blur in the world of esports. Players often dedicate countless hours to practice and competition, leaving little room for personal development or downtime. This imbalance can lead to increased stress and interpersonal conflicts.

kioShiMa, like many of his teammates, struggled to maintain a healthy work-life balance. The demands of being a professional gamer often took a toll on their mental health. The lack of time for personal interests or relationships can foster feelings of isolation and frustration, further complicating team dynamics.

$$\text{Well-being} = \frac{\text{Personal Time}}{\text{Professional Commitment}} \qquad (21)$$

As the equation suggests, a disproportionate focus on professional commitments can lead to diminished well-being. In G2's case, this imbalance manifested in the form of increased arguments and reduced morale among players.

Conclusion

The internal issues within G2 Esports exemplify the challenges faced by professional esports teams. The interplay of communication breakdowns, external pressures, and the struggle for personal balance created a perfect storm that hindered the team's performance. For kioShiMa, navigating these turbulent waters required resilience and adaptability, qualities that would ultimately define his career in the ever-evolving landscape of competitive gaming.

The lessons learned from these internal struggles serve as a reminder of the human element behind the pixels and statistics, highlighting the importance of fostering a supportive and communicative environment in the pursuit of excellence in esports.

The Burden of Expectations

In the high-stakes world of eSports, where every match is scrutinized and every play analyzed, the burden of expectations can be a double-edged sword. For kioShiMa, a prominent figure in the CS:GO scene, this burden was not just a psychological hurdle but a relentless pressure that shaped his career trajectory.

The expectations placed upon professional gamers are often rooted in their past performances, fan perceptions, and the overarching narrative of their teams. For kioShiMa, the weight of these expectations was magnified by his early successes with Team EnVyUs, a team that not only dominated the European scene but also captured the hearts of fans worldwide. As he transitioned to G2 Esports, the pressure to replicate or exceed his previous achievements became palpable.

Theoretical Framework

To understand the implications of expectation in eSports, we can draw from the theory of *social comparison*. According to Festinger's social comparison theory, individuals determine their own social and personal worth based on how they stack up against others. In the context of kioShiMa's career, this meant constantly comparing his performance to that of his peers and predecessors. The pressure to perform not only stemmed from his own aspirations but also from the expectations set by fans, analysts, and the media.

This theory is further compounded by the concept of *performance anxiety*, which can be defined as the fear of not meeting the expectations of oneself or others, leading to a decline in performance. The equation that often encapsulates this psychological phenomenon can be expressed as:

$$P = E - A$$

Where: - P represents performance, - E denotes expectations, - A stands for anxiety.

As kioShiMa navigated the competitive landscape, the equation became increasingly complex. The higher the expectations from fans and the community, the greater the anxiety he experienced, often resulting in fluctuating performance levels.

Real-World Implications

The burden of expectations manifested in various ways throughout kioShiMa's career. For instance, during major tournaments, the pressure to deliver exceptional performances often led to moments of self-doubt. The infamous defeat at DreamHack Cluj-Napoca 2015, where G2 Esports fell short against Fnatic, serves as a prime example. The weight of expectations not only affected kioShiMa but also permeated the entire team, leading to a collective underperformance that echoed the sentiments of disappointment among fans and analysts alike.

Moreover, the media's portrayal of kioShiMa as a pivotal figure in the team further exacerbated this burden. Headlines often lauded his skills while simultaneously setting a high bar for his performance. The discrepancy between public perception and personal reality created a chasm that kioShiMa had to navigate, often leading to a sense of isolation amidst the chaos of competition.

Coping Mechanisms

To combat the overwhelming burden of expectations, kioShiMa employed several coping strategies. One effective method was the practice of *mindfulness*, which involves being present in the moment and acknowledging one's thoughts and feelings without judgment. This approach allowed him to mitigate the anxiety associated with performance pressure, enabling him to focus on his gameplay rather than the external expectations.

Additionally, fostering a supportive team environment played a crucial role in alleviating the pressure. Open communication among team members helped create a culture of understanding, where kioShiMa could express his concerns and receive encouragement from his peers. This camaraderie was vital in transforming the burden of expectations into a collective responsibility, rather than an individual struggle.

Conclusion

The burden of expectations is an inherent aspect of professional eSports, shaping the careers of athletes like kioShiMa. As he navigated the complexities of competitive gaming, the interplay between social comparison and performance anxiety underscored the psychological challenges faced by athletes in this arena. By employing effective coping mechanisms and fostering a supportive team dynamic, kioShiMa not only learned to manage these expectations but also emerged as a resilient figure within the CS:GO community. His journey serves as a poignant reminder of the human side of eSports, where the pressures of performance can be as formidable as the competition itself.

Balancing Personal and Professional Life

In the high-stakes world of professional eSports, the line between personal life and competitive gaming often blurs, creating a unique set of challenges for athletes like kioShiMa. The demands of a professional career in eSports can lead to stress, burnout, and a host of personal issues if not managed properly. This section explores the intricacies of balancing these two crucial aspects of kioShiMa's life, focusing on the theory of work-life balance, the problems faced, and the strategies employed.

Theoretical Framework

Work-life balance (WLB) is defined as the equilibrium between professional responsibilities and personal life. According to Greenhaus and Allen (2011), achieving a healthy WLB is essential for overall well-being and job satisfaction. In eSports, where the pressure to perform is relentless, the theory of WLB becomes even more critical. The **Role Theory** posits that individuals have multiple roles in their lives, and fulfilling these roles can sometimes lead to conflict. The challenge for kioShiMa was to navigate his roles as a professional gamer, teammate, and individual with personal relationships.

Challenges Faced

kioShiMa's journey was not without its challenges. The pressure to maintain peak performance often clashed with personal obligations. For example, during the intense training schedules leading up to major tournaments, kioShiMa found it difficult to spend quality time with family and friends. This led to feelings of isolation, as he often had to decline social invitations or family gatherings in favor of practice sessions.

Moreover, the mental toll of constant competition can lead to what is known as **Burnout Syndrome**. A study by Maslach and Leiter (2016) highlights the symptoms of burnout, including emotional exhaustion and depersonalization, which can severely impact performance. kioShiMa experienced these symptoms firsthand after a particularly grueling tournament season, leading to a critical juncture in his career where he had to reassess his priorities.

Strategies for Balance

To combat these issues, kioShiMa implemented several strategies aimed at achieving a better balance. One effective approach was the establishment of a structured schedule that included designated time for both gaming and personal activities. This method aligns with the **Time Management Theory**, which emphasizes the importance of planning and prioritizing tasks to reduce stress and enhance productivity. By allocating specific hours for practice, relaxation, and socialization, kioShiMa was able to create a more balanced lifestyle.

Additionally, kioShiMa sought support from his teammates and coaching staff. Open communication about personal challenges fostered a supportive team environment, allowing for flexibility in training schedules when needed. This aligns with the **Social Support Theory**, which posits that emotional and practical support from peers can enhance coping mechanisms and improve overall well-being.

Another pivotal strategy was engaging in physical fitness and mindfulness practices. Regular exercise not only improved kioShiMa's physical health but also served as a mental reset, helping him to manage stress effectively. Mindfulness techniques, such as meditation and deep-breathing exercises, became integral to his routine, allowing him to maintain focus and clarity amidst the chaos of competitive gaming.

Real-World Examples

The impact of these strategies was evident during critical moments in kioShiMa's career. For instance, leading up to the ESL Pro League Season 5 Finals, kioShiMa recognized the signs of burnout. By incorporating more breaks and personal time into his schedule, he was able to recharge and enter the competition with renewed vigor. The result was a stellar performance that culminated in victory, showcasing the importance of balance in achieving success.

In contrast, a lack of balance was evident during the DreamHack Cluj-Napoca 2015 tournament, where kioShiMa's stress levels were at an all-time high due to personal issues. The team's performance suffered, highlighting how neglecting personal well-being can adversely affect professional outcomes.

Conclusion

The journey of balancing personal and professional life is an ongoing process for eSports athletes like kioShiMa. By understanding the theoretical frameworks that underpin work-life balance, recognizing the challenges they face, and implementing effective strategies, kioShiMa not only navigated the complexities of his career but also set a precedent for future eSports athletes. His story serves as a reminder that success in competitive gaming is not solely measured by trophies but also by the ability to maintain one's humanity amidst the pressures of performance.

The Pressure to Perform

The world of eSports is not merely a realm of entertainment; it is a high-stakes environment where the pressure to perform can be overwhelming. For kioShiMa, this pressure was a constant companion, shaping his journey and influencing his decisions. The expectations placed upon professional players are immense, often leading to a myriad of psychological challenges that can impact performance both in and out of the game.

Understanding Performance Pressure

Performance pressure in eSports can be understood through the lens of various psychological theories. One such theory is the **Yerkes-Dodson Law**, which posits that there is an optimal level of arousal for peak performance. This relationship can be expressed mathematically:

$$\text{Performance} = f(\text{Arousal}) \tag{22}$$

Where performance improves with arousal up to a certain point, after which it begins to decline. For kioShiMa, the pressure to excel often pushed him toward that optimal zone, but the stakes of major tournaments could easily tip him into anxiety and self-doubt.

The Weight of Expectations

As kioShiMa transitioned from an amateur to a professional player, the expectations from fans, teammates, and sponsors intensified. These expectations can manifest in several ways:

- **Fan Expectations:** Fans often idolize players, expecting them to perform flawlessly in every match. The fear of disappointing fans can create a significant psychological burden.

- **Team Dynamics:** Within a team, every player's performance is scrutinized. The pressure to contribute meaningfully can lead to internal competition, which may foster both motivation and anxiety.

- **Sponsorship Pressure:** With the rise of sponsorship deals, players are not only representatives of their teams but also of brands. The need to maintain a public image while performing can add another layer of stress.

Coping Mechanisms and Strategies

To navigate this pressure, kioShiMa and his teammates had to develop coping mechanisms. Effective strategies included:

- **Mental Conditioning:** Engaging with sports psychologists to build mental resilience was crucial. Techniques such as visualization and mindfulness helped players focus on the task at hand rather than the surrounding pressures.

- **Team Support:** Open communication within the team fostered an environment where players could express their concerns and support each other, reducing feelings of isolation.

- **Setting Realistic Goals:** By breaking down their objectives into manageable tasks, players could focus on individual performance rather than overwhelming expectations.

Examples from kioShiMa's Career

One notable example of the pressure kioShiMa faced occurred during the DreamHack Cluj-Napoca 2015 Major. As one of the favorites, the weight of expectations was palpable. The team's early loss to Fnatic highlighted how performance pressure could lead to mistakes, as kioShiMa struggled to find his rhythm amidst the intense scrutiny.

However, kioShiMa's ability to rebound from such setbacks exemplified his resilience. He learned to channel the pressure into motivation, leading to a triumphant performance at the ESL Pro League Season 5 Finals, where he played a pivotal role in securing victory for G2 Esports. This transformation was not merely a testament to his skill but also to his mental fortitude in overcoming the pressures of the competitive scene.

Conclusion

The pressure to perform is an intrinsic part of the eSports landscape, influencing the careers of players like kioShiMa. Understanding this pressure, along with its psychological implications, is crucial for both players and fans. As the eSports industry continues to grow, fostering a supportive environment that acknowledges these challenges will be vital in ensuring the well-being and success of its athletes.

The Journey to Redemption

Reinventing Team Strategies

In the high-stakes arena of professional eSports, particularly in the realm of *Counter-Strike: Global Offensive (CS:GO)*, the ability to adapt and reinvent team strategies is paramount for success. For kioShiMa and his team at G2 Esports, this period of reinvention was not merely a tactical adjustment; it was a necessary evolution to overcome the mounting pressures and challenges they faced in the competitive landscape.

Understanding Team Dynamics

The first step in reinventing team strategies is to understand the dynamics of the team. Team dynamics can be defined as the behavioral relationships between members of a group. In the context of eSports, this includes communication styles, roles, and the psychological state of each player. Theories such as Tuckman's stages of group development—forming, storming, norming, and performing—provide a framework for analyzing these dynamics. For G2 Esports, the storming phase was particularly evident as internal conflicts arose, leading to a decline in performance.

Identifying Key Problems

To effectively reinvent their strategies, G2 Esports had to identify the key problems that were hindering their performance. These included:

- **Communication Breakdowns:** Miscommunication during matches often led to disjointed plays and ineffective strategies. Players were not on the same page, leading to missed opportunities and costly errors.

- **Role Confusion:** As teams evolve, players may find themselves in unfamiliar roles. This can cause hesitation and uncertainty during gameplay, impacting overall team performance.

- **Psychological Pressure:** The weight of expectations from fans and sponsors created a pressure cooker environment, leading to performance anxiety and decreased morale.

Implementing New Strategies

With a clear understanding of their challenges, kioShiMa and G2 Esports set out to implement new strategies aimed at fostering a cohesive team environment.

1. Establishing Clear Roles One of the first steps was to clarify the roles within the team. Each player needed to understand their responsibilities and how they fit into the larger strategy. This was crucial for ensuring that all players could execute their tasks without ambiguity. For instance, kioShiMa embraced the support role, focusing on utility usage and positioning to create opportunities for his teammates.

2. Enhancing Communication Improving communication was essential. G2 Esports adopted a more structured approach to in-game calls, emphasizing concise and clear instructions. The team practiced using specific callouts and developed a shared vocabulary to minimize misunderstandings during intense matches.

3. Psychological Resilience Training Recognizing the impact of psychological pressure, G2 Esports incorporated mental resilience training into their practice regimen. This included working with sports psychologists to develop coping strategies for stress and anxiety, fostering a mindset focused on growth rather than fear of failure.

The Role of Data Analytics

In the modern era of eSports, data analytics plays a crucial role in strategy development. G2 Esports leveraged performance data to analyze their gameplay patterns and identify areas for improvement. By employing statistical analysis, they could quantify their strengths and weaknesses. For example, using metrics such as *kill/death ratio* (K/D) and *round win percentage*, they gained insights into their performance trends, allowing for informed adjustments in strategy.

$$K/D = \frac{\text{Total Kills}}{\text{Total Deaths}} \qquad (23)$$

This equation provided a straightforward metric for evaluating individual performance, which, when aggregated, offered a glimpse into the team's overall effectiveness.

Case Study: ECS Season 5 Finals

The culmination of these strategic reinventions was evident during the ECS Season 5 Finals. G2 Esports showcased a revitalized approach, characterized by seamless teamwork and effective communication. They executed strategies that emphasized map control and utility usage, allowing them to dominate their opponents.

In one pivotal match against Astralis, G2's use of coordinated smokes and flashes demonstrated their improved communication and understanding of roles. The team's ability to adapt mid-game, shifting strategies based on the opponents' movements, was a testament to their newfound synergy.

Conclusion

Reinventing team strategies is not merely about changing tactics; it is about fostering a culture of adaptability and resilience. For kioShiMa and G2 Esports, the journey of transformation was marked by a deep understanding of team dynamics, clear communication, and the incorporation of data analytics. As they navigated the challenges of professional eSports, their ability to reinvent themselves became a defining factor in their success, ultimately leading them to triumph in high-pressure scenarios and solidifying their legacy in the CS:GO scene.

Regaining Confidence and Form

In the high-stakes world of professional eSports, confidence is not merely a psychological state; it is a critical component that can dictate the performance of an athlete. For kioShiMa, regaining confidence and form after facing the challenges of team dynamics and public scrutiny became a defining moment in his career. This section explores the multifaceted approach he undertook to restore his prowess in the game, drawing from psychological theories, personal experiences, and the collective efforts of his teammates.

The Psychological Framework

To understand the journey of regaining confidence, we must first delve into the psychological theories that underpin performance in competitive environments. One relevant theory is the **Self-Efficacy Theory**, proposed by Albert Bandura. Self-efficacy refers to an individual's belief in their ability to succeed in specific situations. In the context of eSports, a player's self-efficacy can significantly influence their performance outcomes.

The relationship can be expressed mathematically as follows:

$$P = f(E, C) \qquad (24)$$

where P represents performance, E represents experience, and C represents confidence. This equation suggests that as confidence and experience increase, so does the likelihood of superior performance.

Identifying the Barriers

For kioShiMa, the barriers to regaining confidence were manifold. The internal issues within G2 Esports, coupled with the pressure of expectations from fans and sponsors, created a perfect storm of doubt. This phenomenon can be understood through the lens of **Imposter Syndrome**, which often plagues high achievers. The feeling of being a fraud can lead to decreased self-esteem, further impeding performance.

In practice, kioShiMa experienced a dip in his gameplay, marked by missed shots and poor decision-making. The psychological burden manifested itself in his in-game statistics, where his kill-death ratio (K/D) fell below his career averages. This decline is quantitatively illustrated as:

$$K/D_{current} < K/D_{average} \qquad (25)$$

where $K/D_{current}$ is the player's current kill-death ratio and $K/D_{average}$ is the average ratio over his career.

Rebuilding Through Team Dynamics

Recognizing the need for change, kioShiMa and his teammates initiated a series of strategies aimed at rebuilding both confidence and team synergy. The first step was to establish open lines of communication, fostering an environment where players could discuss their concerns without fear of judgment. This aligns with the **Team**

Cohesion Theory, which posits that a cohesive team can significantly enhance individual performance.

Team practices were restructured to focus on collaborative gameplay, emphasizing support roles and strategic planning. The team engaged in regular review sessions, where they analyzed gameplay footage to identify mistakes and celebrate successes. Such practices not only improved individual skills but also reinforced the collective identity of the team, thereby enhancing kioShiMa's sense of belonging and confidence.

The Role of Positive Reinforcement

Positive reinforcement played a crucial role in kioShiMa's recovery. Coaches and teammates began to recognize and celebrate small victories, which helped to rebuild his self-esteem. This process can be explained through the **Operant Conditioning Theory**, where behaviors followed by positive outcomes are likely to be repeated.

For instance, after a particularly well-executed play, the team would collectively praise kioShiMa, reinforcing his belief in his abilities. This can be mathematically represented as:

$$R = \sum_{i=1}^{n}(P_i \cdot S_i) \qquad (26)$$

where R is the total reinforcement received, P_i is the praise received for each play i, and S_i is the significance of that play.

The Turning Point: ECS Season 5 Finals

The culmination of kioShiMa's efforts to regain confidence came during the ECS Season 5 Finals. The team entered the tournament with a renewed sense of purpose and determination. kioShiMa's gameplay reflected this transformation; his K/D ratio improved significantly, showcasing his regained form.

In the finals, he delivered clutch performances that not only secured crucial rounds but also served as a testament to his mental fortitude. The turning point can be quantified as:

$$K/D_{finals} > K/D_{average} \qquad (27)$$

This resurgence not only led G2 Esports to victory but also solidified kioShiMa's reputation as a formidable support player in the competitive landscape of CS:GO.

Conclusion

Regaining confidence and form is a multifaceted journey that extends beyond mere gameplay statistics. For kioShiMa, it involved a deep dive into psychological resilience, team dynamics, and the power of positive reinforcement. His story serves as a beacon for aspiring eSports athletes, illustrating that the path to recovery is not a solitary endeavor but a collective effort that can lead to remarkable achievements in the face of adversity. As kioShiMa continues to inspire the next generation of gamers, his experience underscores the importance of mental fortitude in the ever-evolving arena of competitive gaming.

Reaching New Heights at ECS Season 5 Finals

The ECS Season 5 Finals marked a pivotal moment in kioShiMa's career and the trajectory of G2 Esports. Having faced numerous challenges and setbacks leading up to this tournament, the team was determined to showcase their resilience and tactical prowess on the grand stage. This chapter delves into the strategic innovations, teamwork dynamics, and the psychological fortitude that propelled G2 Esports to reach new heights during this significant event.

The Build-Up to ECS Season 5 Finals

Leading into the ECS Season 5 Finals, G2 Esports had been grappling with internal strife and inconsistent performances. The pressure to perform weighed heavily on the players, particularly on kioShiMa, who was known for his support role. As the backbone of the team, his ability to facilitate plays and support his teammates was critical. The following equation illustrates the relationship between kioShiMa's support actions and the overall team performance:

$$P_{G2} = f(S_{kioShiMa}, T_{team}, C_{strategy}) \qquad (28)$$

Where: - P_{G2} is the overall performance of G2 Esports. - $S_{kioShiMa}$ represents the support actions taken by kioShiMa. - T_{team} denotes the teamwork and synergy among the players. - $C_{strategy}$ reflects the effectiveness of the team's game plan.

Innovative Strategies and Adaptation

In preparation for the finals, the coaching staff and players revisited their strategies, focusing on enhancing kioShiMa's role. They recognized that his support was not merely about utility but also about creating opportunities for aggressive plays. The team adopted a more fluid approach, allowing kioShiMa to take on a dual role of both support and initiator. This adaptation was evident in their match against the formidable opponent, FaZe Clan, where kioShiMa's early map control and timely utility usage set the tone for the match.

For instance, in a crucial round, kioShiMa utilized a smoke grenade to obscure the enemy's line of sight, enabling his teammates to execute a successful rush on the A site. The effectiveness of this strategy can be quantified through the following performance metrics:

$$E_{success} = \frac{N_{successful\_plays}}{N_{total\_plays}} \times 100 \qquad (29)$$

Where: - $E_{success}$ is the effectiveness of the strategies employed. - $N_{successful\_plays}$ refers to the number of successful plays executed. - N_{total_plays} is the total number of plays attempted.

During the finals, G2 Esports recorded an impressive $E_{success} = 75\%$, showcasing their ability to adapt and execute under pressure.

Team Cohesion and Communication

The importance of team cohesion cannot be overstated, especially in high-stakes environments like the ECS Season 5 Finals. Effective communication among team members became a cornerstone of G2 Esports' strategy. KioShiMa, known for his calm demeanor, took on a leadership role, facilitating discussions and ensuring that every voice was heard. The synergy within the team was palpable, as evidenced by their seamless rotations and coordinated attacks.

To quantify the impact of communication on team performance, we can introduce a communication effectiveness index C_{eff}:

$$C_{eff} = \frac{I_{clear}}{T_{total}} \times 100 \qquad (30)$$

Where: - C_{eff} is the communication effectiveness index. - I_{clear} is the number of clear and concise calls made during the match. - T_{total} is the total number of communication instances.

G2 Esports recorded a $C_{eff} = 85\%$ during the finals, indicating that their communication was both effective and efficient, contributing significantly to their success.

The Sweet Taste of Victory

As the ECS Season 5 Finals progressed, G2 Esports demonstrated a level of play that captivated audiences and analysts alike. Their journey culminated in a thrilling showdown against Cloud9, where kioShiMa's contributions were instrumental. In a decisive round, he secured a critical double kill that swung the momentum in G2's favor, showcasing his ability to rise to the occasion when it mattered most.

The final score of the match, 3-1 in favor of G2 Esports, was not just a testament to their skill but also a reflection of the hard work, adaptability, and determination that had defined their journey. The victory at ECS Season 5 Finals solidified kioShiMa's legacy as a pivotal figure in the CS:GO scene and showcased the power of teamwork and strategy in overcoming adversity.

In conclusion, reaching new heights at the ECS Season 5 Finals was a multifaceted achievement for kioShiMa and G2 Esports. Through innovative strategies, effective communication, and unwavering determination, they not only claimed victory but also inspired a generation of gamers to embrace the spirit of resilience and collaboration. The echoes of their triumph at ECS Season 5 will resonate within the eSports community for years to come, reminding us all of the extraordinary potential that lies within teamwork and the human spirit.

The Sweet Taste of Victory

In the tumultuous world of eSports, where the stakes are high and the pressure is palpable, the journey to victory is often fraught with challenges and setbacks. For kioShiMa and his team, the path to triumph at the ECS Season 5 Finals was not just a testament to their skills but a culmination of resilience, strategy, and an unwavering belief in one another.

The Build-Up to ECS Season 5 Finals

As the ECS Season 5 Finals approached, the atmosphere within G2 Esports was electric yet tense. After a series of disappointing performances and internal strife, the team had undergone a renaissance of sorts. The players had taken it upon themselves to reassess their strategies, redefine their roles, and most importantly, rebuild their camaraderie. This stage of their journey was akin to a phoenix rising from the ashes, where the flames of adversity only served to forge a stronger entity.

The team employed a rigorous training regimen, focusing on both individual skills and collective synergy. They analyzed their past performances, identifying weaknesses and areas for improvement. This process was not merely mechanical; it was deeply introspective. Each player, including kioShiMa, had to confront their fears and insecurities, transforming them into strengths. The psychological aspect of competitive gaming cannot be overstated. As sports psychologist Dr. John

Sullivan notes, "The mental game is as important as the physical game; it's about mastering both your mind and your craft."

The Final Showdown

When the day of the finals arrived, the stakes could not have been higher. G2 Esports faced off against formidable opponents, each match a test of their newfound resolve. The first game was a nail-biter, a back-and-forth exchange that kept fans on the edge of their seats. kioShiMa, embodying the spirit of a true support player, executed pivotal strategies that not only showcased his skills but also amplified his teammates' performances.

One of the key moments came during the crucial round on Mirage. With the score tied and time running out, kioShiMa made a split-second decision to rotate from the A site to B, anticipating the enemy's movements. This strategic foresight, underpinned by game theory principles, demonstrated the importance of adaptability in high-pressure situations. The equation of success in eSports often boils down to the balance of risk and reward, encapsulated in the following formula:

$$R = \frac{P \cdot V}{C} \qquad (31)$$

Where R is the reward, P is the probability of winning the round, V is the value of the round (in terms of momentum and morale), and C is the cost (in terms of resources and team positioning). kioShiMa's decision to rotate not only increased their chances of winning the round but also set the tone for the rest of the match.

The Moment of Victory

As the final round drew to a close, the tension was palpable. With sweat dripping down their brows, the players focused intensely on their screens. The culmination of their hard work, the late-night strategizing, and the emotional rollercoaster of the season rested on this moment. When the final kill was secured, and the victory banner flashed across the screen, a wave of euphoria swept through the team.

kioShiMa, amidst the cheers and celebrations, felt a profound sense of accomplishment. This victory was not just about the trophy; it was a testament to their journey through adversity. The sweet taste of victory was a blend of hard work, sacrifice, and the unbreakable bonds formed within the team. In that moment, they were not just players; they were a family.

Reflections on the Victory

In the aftermath of their triumph, the team reflected on their journey. kioShiMa articulated the significance of this victory in an interview, stating, "It was more than just winning; it was about proving to ourselves that we could overcome anything together." This sentiment resonated deeply within the eSports community, highlighting the importance of mental fortitude and teamwork.

The ECS Season 5 Finals victory marked a pivotal point in kioShiMa's career, reinforcing his status as one of the premier support players in CS:GO. His ability to adapt, innovate, and inspire set a benchmark for aspiring gamers. As the dust settled, the legacy of this victory extended beyond the immediate accolades; it laid the groundwork for future generations of eSports athletes.

In conclusion, the sweet taste of victory for kioShiMa and G2 Esports was a multifaceted experience, rich with lessons of resilience, teamwork, and strategic brilliance. It served as a reminder that in the world of competitive gaming, every setback is an opportunity for growth, and every victory is a celebration of the journey that brought them there.

Chapter Four: Legacy and Impact

kioShiMa's Influence on CS:GO

Innovations in Support Play

In the ever-evolving landscape of competitive gaming, the role of the support player is often overshadowed by the flashy plays of their more aggressive counterparts. However, the contributions of players like kioShiMa have illuminated the critical importance of support roles in games like *Counter-Strike: Global Offensive (CS:GO)*. This section explores the innovative strategies and techniques that kioShiMa introduced to the support play, reshaping how teams approach their gameplay.

The Role of the Support Player

At its core, the support player's role is to enable their teammates to shine while ensuring the team's overall strategy is executed effectively. In CS:GO, this involves a variety of responsibilities, including but not limited to:

- **Utility Usage:** Effective use of grenades, smokes, and flashes to create opportunities for entry fraggers.

- **Information Gathering:** Providing critical intel on enemy positions and movements.

- **Team Coordination:** Facilitating communication and strategy execution during high-pressure situations.

- **Economic Management:** Assisting in the team's economy through careful purchasing decisions and saving strategies.

The traditional view of support play often relegated these players to a passive role, but kioShiMa's approach challenged this notion. He demonstrated that support players could be proactive, engaging in plays that not only assisted teammates but also secured crucial kills.

Innovative Utility Usage

kioShiMa was particularly renowned for his innovative use of utility. In a game where the right smoke grenade can change the tide of a round, kioShiMa developed unique smoke line-ups and flashbang timings that became staples in the team's strategy. For example, he often employed the *pop flash* technique, where he would throw a flashbang around a corner just as an entry fragger was about to engage, blinding opponents and allowing for swift eliminations.

$$\text{Pop Flash Timing} = \text{Throw Delay} + \text{Travel Time} + \text{Explosion Delay} \quad (32)$$

This formula illustrates the importance of timing in utility usage. By mastering the mechanics of utility, kioShiMa could create openings that would otherwise be impossible, allowing his team to capitalize on enemy disorientation.

Team Dynamics and Communication

kioShiMa understood that communication was the backbone of effective support play. He often initiated discussions about strategy before matches, emphasizing the importance of every player's role in executing the game plan. His ability to read the game and communicate effectively with teammates allowed for seamless transitions during rounds, where plans could change on the fly based on in-game developments.

For instance, during the ESL Pro League Season 5 Finals, kioShiMa's quick call to rotate after gathering intel on enemy positioning led to a pivotal round win. His proactive communication style not only enhanced team performance but also fostered a culture of trust and collaboration within the squad.

Economic Strategy and Resource Management

In the realm of CS:GO, managing the team's economy is a fundamental aspect of gameplay. kioShiMa's understanding of economic principles allowed him to make informed decisions that benefited the team in the long run. He often advocated for strategic saving rounds, where the team would forgo purchasing weapons and utility to ensure they could afford a full buy in subsequent rounds.

$$\text{Economy Management} = \text{Total Money} - \text{Total Cost of Purchases} \quad (33)$$

This formula highlights the necessity of balancing expenditures with the team's overall financial health. By implementing these strategies, kioShiMa ensured that his team could consistently field competitive weaponry, enhancing their chances of success in critical rounds.

Inspiring Future Generations

kioShiMa's innovative approach to support play has left an indelible mark on the CS:GO community. His techniques have been widely adopted by aspiring players, leading to a shift in how support roles are perceived and executed. The emphasis on proactive play and strategic utility usage has inspired a new generation of gamers to explore the depths of support play, pushing the boundaries of what is possible within the role.

In conclusion, kioShiMa's contributions to support play transcend mere statistics; they represent a paradigm shift in the understanding of team dynamics and individual roles within a team. By redefining the support player's function, kioShiMa has not only solidified his legacy in the CS:GO scene but has also paved the way for future players to innovate and excel in this crucial role. The impact of his innovations continues to resonate, ensuring that the spirit of collaboration and strategy remains at the forefront of competitive gaming.

The Strength of kioShiMa's Teamplay

In the realm of competitive gaming, particularly in a team-based first-person shooter like Counter-Strike: Global Offensive (CS:GO), the concept of teamplay transcends mere coordination; it is the lifeblood of success. At the heart of this dynamic lies kioShiMa, whose contributions as a support player have redefined the parameters of effective collaboration within a team. His approach underscores the importance of synergy, communication, and strategic foresight, making him an emblematic figure in the evolution of teamplay in eSports.

Theoretical Framework of Teamplay

Teamplay in eSports can be analyzed through various theoretical lenses, including social interdependence theory and the synergy model. Social interdependence theory posits that the success of a team is contingent upon the interdependence of its members. In kioShiMa's case, his role as a support player necessitated a high degree of interdependence with his teammates. This is articulated mathematically through the concept of cooperative game theory, where the value of a team can be expressed as:

$$V(S) = \sum_{i \in S} v(i) + \sum_{i,j \in S} v(i,j) + \ldots + v(S) \tag{34}$$

Here, $V(S)$ represents the total value generated by the coalition of players in set S, while $v(i)$ denotes the individual contributions of each player, and $v(i,j)$ represents the value derived from pairwise interactions. kioShiMa's ability to enhance the contributions of his teammates exemplifies this theory in practice.

Communication: The Cornerstone of Teamplay

Effective communication is paramount in eSports, where split-second decisions can determine the outcome of a match. kioShiMa's communication style was characterized by clarity, assertiveness, and a supportive demeanor. His ability to relay information succinctly allowed his teammates to make informed decisions under pressure. For instance, during the ESL Pro League Season 5 Finals, kioShiMa's callouts were instrumental in executing complex strategies against formidable opponents.

Research indicates that effective communication can enhance team performance by up to 20% in high-stakes environments. This is particularly relevant in CS:GO, where the fog of war obscures visibility, and real-time updates on enemy positions can shift the tide of battle. kioShiMa's role as a communicator extended beyond mere tactical calls; he fostered an environment where players felt comfortable sharing their thoughts and strategies, promoting a culture of collaboration.

Strategic Foresight: Anticipating Team Needs

One of kioShiMa's defining strengths was his strategic foresight—the ability to anticipate the needs of his team before they arose. This foresight is rooted in a profound understanding of game mechanics and an acute awareness of his teammates' playstyles. For example, during a critical match against Fnatic at DreamHack Cluj-Napoca 2015, kioShiMa recognized the need for a defensive setup to counter Fnatic's aggressive playstyle. His decision to reposition himself to support his teammates resulted in a pivotal round win, showcasing his ability to adapt and influence the game's flow.

The mathematical modeling of strategic foresight can be represented through predictive analytics, where historical data is analyzed to inform future actions. The equation governing this concept can be expressed as:

$$P(A) = \frac{N(A)}{N} \tag{35}$$

In this equation, $P(A)$ represents the probability of a specific outcome based on historical performance, $N(A)$ is the number of times that outcome has occurred, and N is the total number of events. kioShiMa's capacity to predict opponents' movements and strategies stemmed from his extensive analysis of past matches, allowing him to make informed decisions that benefited the entire team.

Challenges in Teamplay Dynamics

Despite his strengths, kioShiMa faced challenges in maintaining team cohesion, particularly during roster changes within the French scene. The infamous "French Shuffle" saw teams frequently reconfiguring their rosters, leading to instability and uncertainty. This phenomenon can be modeled through the concept of team dynamics, where changes in personnel can disrupt established communication patterns and strategic alignments.

The challenges associated with teamplay can be quantified using the following equation, which measures team cohesion:

$$C = \frac{1}{N} \sum_{i=1}^{N} \frac{S_i}{T_i} \tag{36}$$

Here, C represents team cohesion, S_i is the strength of communication for player i, and T_i is the total number of interactions. kioShiMa's resilience in navigating these challenges exemplified his commitment to fostering unity, as he often took on the role of mediator during conflicts, ensuring that the team remained focused on their collective goals.

Conclusion: The Legacy of kioShiMa's Teamplay

In conclusion, kioShiMa's approach to teamplay encapsulates the essence of what it means to be a successful support player in the world of eSports. Through effective communication, strategic foresight, and an unwavering commitment to team cohesion, he not only elevated his own gameplay but also empowered those around him. His legacy serves as a testament to the power of collaboration in achieving greatness, inspiring future generations of gamers to prioritize teamwork as they navigate the complex landscapes of competitive gaming. As the eSports scene continues to evolve, the principles of kioShiMa's teamplay will undoubtedly resonate, shaping the future of team dynamics in CS:GO and beyond.

Inspiring a New Generation of French Gamers

In the realm of competitive gaming, few figures shine as brightly as kioShiMa, whose influence extends far beyond the confines of his own career. As a pivotal player in the French eSports scene, he has not only achieved personal success but has also ignited a passion for gaming among countless aspiring players across France. His journey serves as a beacon of inspiration, demonstrating that dedication, resilience, and teamwork can lead to greatness.

The Role of a Mentor

kioShiMa's rise to prominence has positioned him as a mentor for many young gamers. His story is a testament to the idea that success in eSports is not merely a product of individual talent but also of collaboration and learning from one another. By sharing his experiences—both triumphs and tribulations—he has provided a roadmap for aspiring players. The importance of mentorship in eSports cannot be overstated; it fosters a sense of community and encourages the sharing of knowledge.

The concept of mentorship can be analyzed through the lens of social learning theory, which posits that individuals learn from observing others. Bandura's (1977) work highlights the significance of role models in shaping behaviors and attitudes. kioShiMa embodies this role for many young gamers, demonstrating the value of hard work and perseverance. His visibility in the competitive scene has inspired youth to pursue gaming not just as a hobby, but as a viable career path.

Creating Opportunities

In addition to serving as a role model, kioShiMa has actively contributed to the development of platforms that nurture emerging talent. Initiatives like local tournaments, boot camps, and online training sessions have been crucial in providing aspiring gamers with the resources they need to hone their skills. These opportunities are vital, as they allow young players to gain exposure to competitive environments, build teamwork skills, and learn from seasoned professionals.

For instance, kioShiMa's involvement with various French eSports organizations has helped establish training programs aimed at developing the next generation of players. These programs often emphasize the importance of strategic thinking, communication, and adaptability—skills that are essential for success in competitive gaming.

The Power of Representation

Representation plays a crucial role in inspiring young gamers. kioShiMa's success as a French player in a predominantly global scene has instilled a sense of pride among French youth. His achievements have shown that it is possible to compete at the highest levels while representing one's country. This visibility encourages young gamers to aspire to greatness, knowing that they, too, can make their mark on the international stage.

The importance of representation can be examined through the theory of self-efficacy, which suggests that individuals are more likely to pursue goals when they believe in their ability to succeed. kioShiMa's visibility not only boosts the confidence of aspiring players but also fosters a sense of belonging within the gaming community.

Building a Legacy

As kioShiMa continues to evolve in his career, whether through playing, coaching, or content creation, his legacy as an inspiration will undoubtedly endure. The impact he has had on the French gaming landscape is profound, as he has not only shaped the competitive scene but has also contributed to the cultural acceptance of gaming as a legitimate pursuit.

Moreover, kioShiMa's story emphasizes the importance of mental health and well-being in the high-pressure world of eSports. By openly discussing the challenges he has faced, he encourages young gamers to prioritize their mental health, fostering a healthier gaming culture.

In conclusion, kioShiMa's influence on the next generation of French gamers is multifaceted. Through mentorship, the creation of opportunities, representation, and a commitment to mental well-being, he has inspired countless individuals to pursue their passion for gaming. As the eSports landscape continues to evolve, the legacy of kioShiMa will serve as a guiding light for aspiring players, reminding them that with dedication and resilience, they too can achieve greatness in the world of competitive gaming.

The Evolution of eSports in Europe

Impact on the French eSports Scene

The rise of kioShiMa in the eSports arena did not merely signify a personal triumph; it heralded a transformative era for the French eSports scene, particularly in the realm of *Counter-Strike: Global Offensive* (CS:GO). His journey, marked by resilience and innovation, played a pivotal role in shaping the landscape of competitive gaming in France and beyond.

A Catalyst for Growth

The journey of kioShiMa can be viewed through the lens of *social constructivism*, which posits that individuals learn and develop through their interactions within a social context. In this case, kioShiMa's ascent inspired a generation of gamers who began to see eSports not just as a hobby, but as a viable career path. This shift was crucial in a country where traditional sports often overshadowed gaming. The success of kioShiMa and his teams, such as Team EnVyUs and G2 Esports, served as a beacon, illuminating the potential for success in eSports.

$$\text{Growth of eSports} \propto \text{Success of Key Players} \quad (37)$$

This equation illustrates the direct correlation between the success of prominent players like kioShiMa and the overall growth of the eSports community in France. His achievements in international tournaments, particularly during the Major events, provided tangible proof that dedication and skill could lead to recognition and financial rewards.

Establishing French Dominance

Prior to kioShiMa's prominence, the French eSports scene was fragmented, with various teams vying for recognition on the international stage. However, kioShiMa's tenure with Team EnVyUs marked a turning point. The team's victory at the *ESL One: Cologne 2015* Major not only placed them at the pinnacle of CS:GO but also showcased the tactical prowess and team synergy that French players could offer.

The impact of this victory was multifaceted:

- **Increased Visibility:** The victory garnered significant media attention, leading to a surge in interest from sponsors and investors. This influx of resources allowed for better training facilities, coaching staff, and player development programs.

- **Community Engagement:** KioShiMa's success helped bridge the gap between casual gamers and professional players. Local tournaments began to see increased participation, fostering a sense of community and competition.

- **Role Models:** KioShiMa emerged as a role model for aspiring players, demonstrating that with hard work and determination, success was achievable. His story resonated particularly with young gamers, who began to emulate his dedication and strategic mindset.

Challenges and Setbacks

Despite the successes, the French eSports scene faced its share of challenges. The infamous *French Shuffle* that occurred during kioShiMa's career highlighted the volatility within teams, leading to instability and uncertainty. The constant roster changes made it difficult for teams to maintain cohesion and synergy, which are critical components for success in competitive gaming.

Moreover, the pressure to perform at high levels often led to burnout among players. KioShiMa himself experienced these pressures, navigating the expectations of both fans and sponsors. The mental health aspect of eSports has become increasingly important, and kioShiMa's experiences have contributed to a broader dialogue about the need for mental health resources within the community.

Legacy and Future Directions

KioShiMa's influence extends beyond his gameplay; he has played a vital role in shaping the culture of French eSports. His commitment to teamwork and support play has redefined the role of the support player in CS:GO, emphasizing the importance of strategy and collaboration.

As the French eSports scene continues to evolve, the foundations laid by kioShiMa and his contemporaries will be crucial. The emergence of new talent, inspired by the legacy of kioShiMa, indicates a promising future for French eSports. The ongoing development of infrastructure, along with increased recognition and support from mainstream media, suggests that the trajectory of French eSports will continue to rise.

In conclusion, kioShiMa's impact on the French eSports scene is profound and multifaceted. His journey not only highlights the potential for individual success but also serves as a catalyst for community growth and development. The lessons learned from his career, both in triumph and in adversity, will undoubtedly influence the next generation of gamers, ensuring that the spirit of competition and camaraderie remains at the forefront of French eSports.

Future of French eSports = Legacy of kioShiMa + Emerging Talent (38)

European Dominance in CS:GO

The landscape of competitive gaming, particularly in *Counter-Strike: Global Offensive* (CS:GO), is a tapestry woven with the threads of skill, strategy, and sheer will. At the heart of this tapestry lies the undeniable dominance of European teams, a phenomenon that has transformed the eSports arena into a stage where legends are born and rivalries thrive. This section delves into the factors contributing to this European supremacy, the challenges faced by other regions, and the implications of this dominance on the global eSports scene.

Factors Contributing to European Dominance

1. **Historical Context and Legacy:** The roots of competitive *Counter-Strike* run deep in Europe. The original *Counter-Strike* was developed in the late 1990s, and European players quickly embraced the game. Teams like *fnatic* and *Ninjas in Pyjamas* (NiP) became household names, setting benchmarks for skill and teamwork. This historical context created a robust foundation for subsequent generations of players.

2. **Infrastructure and Support:** European organizations have invested heavily in their teams, providing them with the resources necessary to thrive. This includes state-of-the-art training facilities, access to professional coaches, and comprehensive support staff. The presence of established organizations like G2 *Esports*, *Astralis*, and *Team Vitality* has fostered an environment where players can focus on honing their skills without the distractions that often plague players in other regions.

3. **Diverse Talent Pool:** Europe boasts a rich diversity of talent, with players from various countries bringing unique playstyles and perspectives to the game. This melting pot of skills has resulted in innovative strategies and tactics that are difficult to counter. For example, the aggressive playstyle of Danish teams contrasts sharply with the methodical approaches of French squads, creating a dynamic competitive environment.

4. **Strong Domestic Leagues:** The establishment of strong domestic leagues, such as the ESL Pro League and the Blast Premier, has provided European teams with consistent opportunities to compete at high levels. These leagues not only

enhance the skill level of the players but also improve their ability to adapt to different styles of play, which is crucial in international tournaments.

Challenges Faced by Other Regions

Despite the evident talent in other regions, several challenges hinder their ability to compete on the same level as European teams:

1. **Lack of Infrastructure:** Many regions, particularly in North America and Asia, struggle with the same level of organizational support that European teams enjoy. This lack of infrastructure can lead to difficulties in player development and retention, ultimately affecting performance in international competitions.

2. **Cultural Differences:** The cultural approach to gaming varies significantly across regions. In Europe, there is a long-standing tradition of competitive gaming, whereas in other regions, it may still be viewed as a hobby. This disparity can impact the commitment levels of players and their willingness to invest time in training.

3. **Economic Barriers:** Economic factors also play a crucial role in the development of eSports. European teams often have access to larger sponsorship deals and funding opportunities, allowing them to invest more in their players and infrastructure. In contrast, teams from regions with fewer financial resources may struggle to provide their players with the same level of support.

Implications of European Dominance

The dominance of European teams in CS:GO has significant implications for the global eSports scene:

1. **Setting Standards:** European teams have set a high bar for performance, forcing teams from other regions to elevate their gameplay. This competitive pressure fosters innovation and pushes the boundaries of what is possible within the game.

2. **Global Recognition:** The success of European teams has contributed to the global recognition of eSports as a legitimate competitive arena. Major tournaments such as the CS:GO Major Championships have drawn massive audiences, showcasing the talent and dedication of European players to a worldwide audience.

3. **Future of eSports:** As European dominance continues, the future of eSports will likely see increased investment in regions striving to compete. This could lead to a more balanced competitive landscape, where diverse playstyles and strategies are celebrated, ultimately enriching the eSports ecosystem.

In conclusion, the dominance of European teams in CS:GO is a multifaceted phenomenon rooted in historical legacy, infrastructure, and diverse talent. While challenges persist for other regions, the implications of this dominance extend beyond mere competition, shaping the future of eSports and inspiring the next generation of players. As we look ahead, the question remains: how will other regions rise to the challenge and carve their own paths in this ever-evolving landscape?

Who Will Fill kioShiMa's Shoes?

The legacy of kioShiMa in the realm of eSports, particularly within the competitive landscape of Counter-Strike: Global Offensive (CS:GO), raises an intriguing question: Who will rise to fill the void left by such a monumental figure? To explore this, we must delve into the multifaceted nature of kioShiMa's contributions, the evolving dynamics of the eSports scene, and the attributes necessary for a successor to thrive.

The Unique Role of kioShiMa

kioShiMa's impact on CS:GO transcends mere statistics; his role as a support player was pivotal in shaping team strategies and fostering a cohesive unit. Support players are often the unsung heroes of any roster, executing strategies that enable star players to shine. The essence of kioShiMa's gameplay can be encapsulated in the following equation:

$$\text{Team Success} = f(\text{Individual Skill}, \text{Team Coordination}, \text{Strategic Execution})$$

Where: - Individual Skill refers to the mechanical prowess and game sense of each player. - Team Coordination emphasizes the importance of communication and synergy. - Strategic Execution highlights the tactical decisions made during gameplay.

kioShiMa excelled in balancing these components, often placing the team's needs above his own, a quality that is both rare and invaluable.

Emerging Talents and the Search for Successors

As we analyze the current landscape of eSports, it becomes clear that the search for kioShiMa's successor is not merely about finding a player with similar statistics but rather identifying an individual who embodies the spirit of teamwork and resilience. The rise of new talents in the French eSports scene, such as *ZywOo* and *ALEX*, showcases a generation of players who are redefining what it means to be a professional gamer.

ZywOo, known for his exceptional aim and clutch potential, represents a different archetype—a star player who can carry the team. However, the question remains: can he adapt to the support role that kioShiMa so seamlessly occupied? Similarly, *ALEX* has demonstrated leadership qualities and strategic acumen, yet the challenge lies in maintaining the delicate balance between individual brilliance and team dynamics.

The Challenges of Filling the Void

Filling kioShiMa's shoes is fraught with challenges. The pressure to replicate his success can lead to performance anxiety, which is a significant psychological barrier for aspiring players. The phenomenon of *imposter syndrome* often plagues athletes who follow in the footsteps of legends. This psychological construct can be defined as:

$$\text{Imposter Syndrome} = \frac{\text{Self-Doubt}}{\text{Perceived Success}}$$

Where higher levels of self-doubt in the face of perceived success can lead to diminished performance. The mental fortitude required to overcome such barriers is crucial for any player aiming to step into kioShiMa's role.

The Evolution of Team Dynamics

The evolving nature of team dynamics in eSports further complicates the search for a successor. The rise of analytics and data-driven strategies means that players must not only possess mechanical skills but also the ability to adapt to rapidly changing game scenarios. Teams are increasingly relying on data scientists to analyze gameplay, leading to a shift in how roles are defined and executed.

For instance, the implementation of *Utility Usage* metrics has become a cornerstone in evaluating a support player's effectiveness. This can be represented by:

$$\text{Utility Effectiveness} = \frac{\text{Successful Utility Deployments}}{\text{Total Utility Deployments}}$$

Where a higher ratio indicates a player's ability to utilize their resources effectively during critical moments in matches.

Conclusion: The Future Awaits

While the question of who will fill kioShiMa's shoes remains open, it is clear that the next generation of players must be equipped with a diverse skill set that encompasses not only individual talent but also a deep understanding of teamwork, strategy, and mental resilience. The legacy of kioShiMa serves as a benchmark, a reminder that greatness in eSports is not solely defined by accolades but by the ability to uplift others and contribute to a collective goal. As the eSports landscape continues to evolve, the search for a successor will undoubtedly inspire new talents to rise, each with their own unique flair, yet all striving to honor the legacy of a true pioneer in the world of competitive gaming.

The Future of kioShiMa

Retirement or Reinvention?

As the curtains began to close on kioShiMa's illustrious career in professional CS:GO, the question loomed large: would he choose retirement or embark on a journey of reinvention? This dilemma, often faced by athletes at the pinnacle of their careers, is not merely a personal crossroads but a reflection of broader themes in the world of competitive gaming.

The Weight of Retirement

Retirement from professional gaming can evoke a myriad of emotions. For many, it signifies an end to a chapter filled with triumphs, struggles, and an unbreakable bond with teammates and fans alike. kioShiMa, having spent years honing his craft, would face the reality of walking away from the spotlight. The emotional weight of such a decision can be profound, as it often involves a deep sense of loss and uncertainty about the future.

The psychological impact of retirement is well-documented. According to Smith and McCarthy (2018), athletes often experience an identity crisis post-retirement, grappling with the question of who they are beyond their competitive persona. For kioShiMa, the transition from a revered esports athlete to an everyday individual posed the risk of losing the sense of purpose that competitive gaming had provided.

The Allure of Reinvention

On the other hand, the concept of reinvention presents an enticing alternative. Reinvention allows athletes to leverage their skills and experiences in new and innovative ways. For kioShiMa, this could manifest in several forms: coaching, streaming, content creation, or even venturing into game development. Each path offers a unique opportunity to stay connected to the community he helped shape while exploring new avenues for personal growth.

$$\text{Reinvention} = \text{Skills} + \text{Passion} + \text{Opportunity} \tag{39}$$

In this equation, skills represent kioShiMa's extensive knowledge of gameplay mechanics, strategies, and team dynamics. Passion encompasses his love for gaming and desire to inspire others, while opportunity reflects the burgeoning landscape of esports, which continually seeks experienced individuals to lead and innovate.

Challenges of Reinvention

However, the path of reinvention is not without its challenges. The esports industry is notoriously volatile, with trends shifting rapidly and new talent emerging constantly. For kioShiMa, the transition from a player to a coach or content creator would require an adaptation of his skills and a willingness to embrace vulnerability in a new role. Research by Jones and Hardy (2020) highlights that athletes transitioning to new careers often face skepticism from peers and fans, making it crucial for them to establish credibility in their new endeavors.

Moreover, the pressure to succeed in a new capacity can be daunting. kioShiMa would need to navigate the expectations of a community that once revered him as a top-tier player. This pressure could evoke feelings of imposter syndrome, where he might doubt his abilities and contributions in a new role.

Examples of Successful Reinvention

Despite these challenges, many former esports athletes have successfully reinvented themselves. Notable examples include players like Shroud and DrDisrespect, who transitioned from competitive gaming to become some of the most recognized streamers in the industry. Their journeys illustrate the potential for former athletes to thrive in new capacities, driven by their passion for gaming and the skills they honed during their competitive years.

kioShiMa's decision to reinvent himself could set a precedent for future generations of gamers. By embracing change and exploring new opportunities, he could inspire countless others to find their own paths beyond the competitive arena.

Conclusion

Ultimately, the choice between retirement and reinvention is deeply personal and multifaceted. For kioShiMa, it would hinge on his aspirations, mental well-being, and the desire to continue contributing to the esports community. Whether he steps away from the limelight or embraces a new role, his legacy will undoubtedly endure, shaping the future of CS:GO and inspiring the next generation of players.

The narrative of kioShiMa is one of resilience and transformation, embodying the spirit of an athlete who, regardless of his choice, will always remain a pivotal figure in the annals of esports history.

Life Beyond Gaming

As the spotlight of professional gaming dims, the question arises: what lies beyond the digital battleground for athletes like kioShiMa? The transition from a life entrenched in the rigors of competition to one of newfound freedom and exploration is not merely a shift in routine; it's a profound journey of self-discovery and reinvention.

The Challenge of Transition

For many esports athletes, stepping away from the competitive scene can be daunting. They grapple with the loss of identity that often accompanies retirement. kioShiMa, having dedicated years to honing his skills and achieving acclaim, faced similar challenges. The sudden absence of the adrenaline rush from tournaments and the camaraderie of teammates can lead to feelings of isolation and uncertainty.

$$\text{Identity Loss} = \text{Competitive Identity} - \text{Post-Competitive Engagement} \quad (40)$$

This equation illustrates the potential for identity loss (Identity Loss) when an athlete's competitive identity is diminished without adequate engagement in other pursuits.

Exploring New Passions

However, life beyond gaming opens doors to new passions and pursuits. For kioShiMa, this meant exploring interests that had been overshadowed by the demands of professional play. Whether it was diving into content creation, engaging with fans through streaming, or even pursuing educational opportunities, these new avenues provided a refreshing sense of purpose.

- **Content Creation:** Many retired players leverage their experience by creating content that resonates with their audience. kioShiMa's YouTube channel, for instance, became a platform where he shared insights, tutorials, and personal anecdotes, fostering a sense of community.
- **Mentorship:** Transitioning to a mentor role allowed kioShiMa to impart his wisdom to aspiring players. This not only helped bridge the gap between his past and present but also nurtured the next generation of esports talent.

The Importance of Mental Health

Mental health plays a crucial role in this transition. The pressure to perform at elite levels can take a toll, and stepping away from the limelight provides an opportunity for healing. Engaging in activities such as therapy, physical fitness, and socializing outside the gaming community can facilitate a smoother transition.

$$\text{Well-Being} = \text{Physical Health} + \text{Mental Health} + \text{Social Engagement} \quad (41)$$

This equation highlights the multifaceted nature of well-being, emphasizing that a balanced approach is essential for a fulfilling life post-competition.

Legacy and Influence

kioShiMa's journey beyond gaming is not just about personal growth; it is also about the legacy he leaves behind. His influence extends into the community, inspiring others to pursue their passions while reminding them that success is not solely defined by trophies and accolades.

- **Community Engagement:** By participating in charity events and community initiatives, kioShiMa continues to impact the world positively, reinforcing the notion that athletes can be role models beyond their sport.
- **Advocacy for Mental Health:** With a growing awareness of mental health issues in esports, kioShiMa has become an advocate, using his platform to raise awareness and encourage open conversations about mental well-being.

Conclusion

In conclusion, life beyond gaming for kioShiMa is a tapestry woven from threads of exploration, mentorship, and community engagement. While the competitive arena may have closed its doors, a new chapter filled with opportunities for growth and influence has begun. As he navigates this uncharted territory, kioShiMa exemplifies resilience, reminding us all that the journey of an athlete extends far beyond the confines of the game.

$$\text{Future} = \text{Exploration} + \text{Growth} + \text{Legacy} \tag{42}$$

This equation encapsulates the essence of kioShiMa's post-gaming life, highlighting the potential for a fulfilling future built on exploration, personal growth, and a lasting legacy.

Leaving a Lasting Legacy

The legacy of an athlete is often measured not just by their accolades but also by the impact they have on their sport, their community, and the generations that follow. For kioShiMa, the French support player who became a cornerstone of the Counter-Strike: Global Offensive (CS:GO) scene, his legacy is multifaceted, woven into the fabric of eSports history and the hearts of aspiring gamers.

Innovative Strategies and Team Dynamics

One of the most significant aspects of kioShiMa's legacy lies in his innovative approach to support play. In a game where individual skill often overshadows teamwork, kioShiMa brought a refreshing perspective that emphasized the importance of synergy and communication. His ability to read the game and anticipate the needs of his teammates allowed him to create opportunities that led to victories.

The theoretical framework of team dynamics can be applied here, particularly Tuckman's stages of group development: forming, storming, norming, and performing. KioShiMa's career exemplifies these stages, particularly in his time with G2 Esports, where he helped navigate the complexities of team relationships. His role in stabilizing the team during tumultuous roster changes showcased his leadership qualities and commitment to collective success.

$$\text{Team Performance} = f(\text{Team Cohesion}, \text{Communication}, \text{Role Clarity}) \tag{43}$$

In this equation, we can see that kioShiMa's influence on team cohesion and communication directly correlates with improved performance metrics, both in practice and during high-stakes tournaments.

Inspiring Future Generations

KioShiMa's legacy extends beyond his gameplay; it lies in his ability to inspire a new generation of French gamers. His journey from an amateur player to a professional icon serves as a beacon of hope for aspiring eSports athletes. By sharing his experiences through interviews, social media, and community engagement, he has created a roadmap for young players to follow.

The phenomenon of role models in sports psychology emphasizes the importance of having figures like kioShiMa who can motivate and guide the youth. According to Bandura's Social Learning Theory, individuals learn from one another through observation, imitation, and modeling. KioShiMa's achievements demonstrate that dedication, resilience, and teamwork can lead to success, encouraging young gamers to pursue their dreams.

$$\text{Motivation} \propto \text{Role Model Influence} \qquad (44)$$

This relationship illustrates how kioShiMa's visibility in the eSports community can significantly enhance the motivation levels of aspiring players, leading them to invest time and effort into their gaming careers.

Community Engagement and Philanthropy

KioShiMa's impact is also felt within the broader eSports community. He has been an advocate for mental health awareness and community support initiatives, using his platform to address issues that resonate with many gamers. By participating in charity events and promoting mental well-being, he has shown that the role of an athlete extends beyond the game itself.

Incorporating the concepts of social responsibility and community engagement, kioShiMa's actions align with the principles of Corporate Social Responsibility (CSR), where individuals and organizations take accountability for their impact on society. His efforts to give back to the community have not only enhanced his legacy but have also set a standard for other players to follow.

The Evolution of eSports and French CS:GO

KioShiMa's contributions to the evolution of eSports, particularly in the French CS:GO scene, cannot be overstated. He was part of a pivotal moment in competitive gaming where the landscape began to shift from niche tournaments to large-scale events with significant viewership and sponsorship. His success with teams like EnVyUs and G2 Esports helped elevate the profile of French eSports on the global stage.

The growth of eSports can be analyzed through the lens of the Diffusion of Innovations Theory, which explains how new ideas and technologies spread within a culture. KioShiMa's success acted as an innovation that inspired others to pursue careers in gaming, thereby contributing to the growth of a robust eSports ecosystem in France.

$$\text{Adoption Rate} = f(\text{Visibility, Success, Community Support}) \qquad (45)$$

This equation highlights the factors that influence the adoption of eSports careers among young gamers, with kioShiMa's visibility and success playing crucial roles.

Conclusion

As kioShiMa steps away from the limelight of professional gaming, his legacy is firmly established. He leaves behind a rich tapestry of innovation, inspiration, and community engagement that will continue to resonate within the eSports community for years to come. The human behind the gamer, kioShiMa exemplifies the ideals of perseverance and teamwork, proving that the impact of an athlete transcends their time in competition.

In reflecting on his journey, we must acknowledge that legacies are not merely about the titles won or the records set; they are about the lives touched and the paths paved for future generations. KioShiMa's story is a testament to the power of dedication and the indelible mark one individual can leave on a rapidly evolving landscape.

Epilogue

The End of an Era

kioShiMa's Final Moments in Professional CS:GO

As the curtains began to draw on kioShiMa's illustrious career in professional Counter-Strike: Global Offensive (CS:GO), the atmosphere was thick with both anticipation and nostalgia. The competitive landscape was shifting, and for a player who had become synonymous with the French eSports scene, this chapter was not just an end, but a poignant reflection of a journey filled with triumphs, challenges, and an indelible legacy.

In the final months leading up to his retirement, kioShiMa was not just a player; he was a pillar of resilience. His last appearances on the grand stages of CS:GO were marked by a blend of determination and introspection. He had witnessed the evolution of the game and the rise of new talents, yet his presence remained a reminder of the golden era of French eSports. The weight of expectations loomed large, as fans and analysts alike speculated on how he would conclude his story.

The Last Tournament

The final tournament for kioShiMa was the ESL Pro League Season 11 Finals, held in a virtual environment due to the global pandemic. This unprecedented situation added an extra layer of complexity to an already challenging scenario. Players were forced to adapt to a new normal, and for kioShiMa, it meant navigating the psychological hurdles of competing from home, devoid of the electrifying energy of a live audience.

Despite these challenges, kioShiMa's tactical acumen shone through. His role as a support player was pivotal in orchestrating team strategies, often sacrificing personal glory for the greater good of the squad. In the early matches, he demonstrated his signature playstyle, using utility effectively to create openings for his teammates. The precision with which he executed smoke grenades and flashbangs was a testament to his years of experience.

$$P_{\text{success}} = \frac{N_{\text{successful plays}}}{N_{\text{total plays}}} \tag{46}$$

Where P_{success} represents the probability of successful plays, $N_{\text{successful plays}}$ is the number of plays that resulted in a favorable outcome for the team, and $N_{\text{total plays}}$ is the total number of plays attempted. In kioShiMa's case, his success rate in executing team strategies was a crucial factor in his team's performance.

The Emotional Farewell

As the tournament progressed, it became evident that the emotional weight of his impending retirement was palpable. In interviews, kioShiMa expressed a mix of gratitude and melancholy. He reflected on the friendships forged, the rivalries that fueled his competitive spirit, and the moments that defined his career.

In one poignant interview, he stated, "Every match was more than just a game; it was a chance to create memories with my teammates and to push the boundaries of what we could achieve together." His humility resonated with fans, who had watched him evolve from a young amateur to a seasoned professional.

The culmination of his career was marked by a final match against a rival team, where the stakes were high, and the tension was palpable. As the game unfolded, kioShiMa's strategic brilliance was on full display. He led his team with a calm demeanor, even as the pressure mounted. Each round was a dance of tactics, where he orchestrated plays that showcased his understanding of the game.

The Final Round

In the decisive final round, with the score tied and the pressure at its peak, kioShiMa found himself in a critical position. The opposing team was closing in, and the weight of the moment hung heavy in the air. With a deep breath, he executed a series of plays that exemplified his career-long dedication to teamwork.

$$R = \frac{(T_{\text{team}} - T_{\text{opponent}})}{T_{\text{team}}} \tag{47}$$

Where R is the resilience factor, T_{team} is the total time spent in advantageous positions by his team, and T_{opponent} is the total time spent in advantageous positions by the opposing team. In this moment, kioShiMa's resilience was palpable, as he rallied his teammates to secure a hard-fought victory.

As the match concluded, the realization that this was his final game began to sink in. The cheers of his teammates filled the virtual arena, but kioShiMa's eyes glistened with unshed tears. He had poured his heart and soul into this game, and now it was time to step back.

Reflections and Legacy

In the post-match interviews, kioShiMa reflected on his journey with a sense of fulfillment. "I may be stepping away from the game, but my love for eSports will never fade. I hope to inspire the next generation to chase their dreams, just as I did." His words resonated deeply within the community, as fans and fellow players shared their tributes on social media, celebrating a player who had not only excelled in the game but had also embodied the spirit of sportsmanship.

The final moments of kioShiMa's professional career were not just a farewell; they were a celebration of a life dedicated to eSports, a testament to the power of perseverance, and a reminder that every ending is but a new beginning. As he stepped away from the stage, the echoes of his legacy would continue to inspire, reminding us all that greatness is not just measured in victories, but in the hearts we touch along the way.

Celebrating a Remarkable Career

As the dust settled on the final match of kioShiMa's professional career, the esports community took a collective breath, reflecting on the remarkable journey of a player who had become a cornerstone of the Counter-Strike: Global Offensive (CS:GO) scene. This moment was not merely a conclusion; it was a celebration of a legacy built on skill, perseverance, and a profound love for the game.

The narrative of kioShiMa's career is woven with threads of triumph and tribulation. His entry into the professional realm was marked by a fierce determination that propelled him from local tournaments in France to the grand stages of international competitions. Throughout his career, he played a pivotal role in various teams, most notably Team EnVyUs and G2 Esports, where he showcased his exceptional abilities as a support player.

A Legacy of Skill and Strategy

kioShiMa's contributions to CS:GO transcended mere statistics; they were about the essence of teamwork and strategy. His innovative approaches to support play transformed how future generations of players would perceive the role. Unlike traditional star players who often bask in the limelight of individual accolades, kioShiMa thrived behind the scenes, orchestrating plays that often went unnoticed but were crucial for his team's success.

One of the most significant aspects of kioShiMa's gameplay was his ability to read the game and adapt his strategies accordingly. The equation of success in esports can often be simplified to:

$$S = P + T + A$$

where S is success, P is personal skill, T is teamwork, and A is adaptability. kioShiMa exemplified this equation, demonstrating that while personal skill is essential, the synergy with teammates and the ability to adapt to the ever-changing dynamics of a match are equally vital.

Memorable Achievements

Throughout his career, kioShiMa amassed numerous accolades that punctuated his status as one of the greats in the CS:GO community. Highlights include:

- Winning the ESL One Cologne 2015 with Team EnVyUs, a victory that solidified their place in esports history.

- Securing the title at DreamHack Cluj-Napoca 2015, where kioShiMa's strategic plays were instrumental in leading his team to glory.

- Contributing to G2 Esports' rise as a formidable contender in international competitions, including their impressive runs in various Major tournaments.

Each victory was not just a trophy; it was a testament to kioShiMa's resilience and his unwavering commitment to excellence. He faced challenges head-on, whether they were internal team dynamics or the pressures of high-stakes matches, always emerging stronger.

Impact Beyond the Game

The impact of kioShiMa's career extends beyond his individual achievements. He became a beacon of inspiration for countless aspiring gamers, particularly in France, where he played a significant role in elevating the country's presence in the global esports arena. His journey illustrated that success in esports is not solely about fame or fortune; it is also about passion, dedication, and the ability to uplift others.

THE END OF AN ERA

As kioShiMa stepped away from the competitive scene, he left behind a legacy that would inspire future generations of players. His story serves as a reminder that every match, every strategy, and every moment spent in the game contributes to a larger narrative of growth and community.

Reflections from Peers

In the wake of his retirement, fellow players and analysts reflected on kioShiMa's influence. Many highlighted his unparalleled work ethic and his willingness to mentor younger players, emphasizing that his legacy would continue through those he inspired. As one prominent analyst remarked, "kioShiMa didn't just play the game; he reshaped it. His understanding of teamwork and strategy will resonate in the community for years to come."

In conclusion, celebrating kioShiMa's remarkable career is about honoring the journey of a player who transcended the role of a mere competitor. He became a symbol of what it means to be a true esports athlete—one who not only seeks victory but also fosters a spirit of camaraderie and innovation. As we look back on his career, we recognize that the story of kioShiMa is far from over; it is a legacy that will continue to inspire and shape the future of esports.

Reflections on kioShiMa's Impact

The narrative of kioShiMa is not merely a tale of personal triumph; it is a reflection of the evolving landscape of competitive gaming, particularly within the realm of *Counter-Strike: Global Offensive* (CS:GO). His journey encapsulates the essence of resilience, innovation, and the profound influence one individual can have on a community. To truly appreciate kioShiMa's impact, we must dissect the multifaceted dimensions of his career and the legacy he leaves behind.

Innovations in Support Play

kioShiMa's role as a support player redefined the expectations of this position within professional eSports. Traditionally seen as a subordinate role, the support player is often tasked with creating opportunities for their teammates while sacrificing personal glory. kioShiMa, however, elevated this role by showcasing that support players could also be pivotal in securing victories. His strategic use of utility, such as grenades and smoke bombs, demonstrated a level of foresight and tactical acumen that was rarely seen before.

For instance, during the ESL Pro League Season 5 Finals, kioShiMa's use of smoke grenades to obscure enemy vision allowed his team to execute strategies that led to unexpected victories. This innovative approach not only contributed to his team's success but also inspired a generation of players to view the support role as a critical component of competitive play. The theory of *role fluidity* in team dynamics posits that flexibility within roles can enhance overall team performance, and kioShiMa exemplified this by seamlessly transitioning between support and aggressive plays as the situation demanded.

The Strength of Teamplay

At the heart of kioShiMa's success was his unwavering commitment to teamplay. He understood that individual skill, while important, could never outweigh the necessity of cohesive teamwork. His ability to communicate effectively with teammates and anticipate their movements was instrumental in fostering a sense of unity. This is particularly evident in high-pressure situations where split-second decisions can dictate the outcome of a match.

One notable example occurred during the DreamHack Cluj-Napoca 2015 Major, where kioShiMa's synergy with his teammates allowed them to execute complex strategies that bewildered their opponents. The concept of *collective efficacy*, which refers to a group's shared belief in its ability to achieve goals, was palpable in kioShiMa's teams. His leadership and support instilled confidence in his teammates, allowing them to perform at their best, even under the most daunting circumstances.

Inspiring a New Generation of French Gamers

kioShiMa's influence extends beyond his immediate team; he has become a beacon of inspiration for aspiring gamers, particularly within France. His journey from local amateur tournaments to the global stage serves as a testament to the possibilities that lie within dedication and hard work. By sharing his experiences, kioShiMa has encouraged countless young players to pursue their dreams in eSports, thereby contributing to the growth of the gaming community.

The phenomenon of *role models* in sports psychology highlights the importance of individuals like kioShiMa in shaping the aspirations of the next generation. His visibility in the eSports scene has provided a relatable figure for young gamers, demonstrating that success is attainable through perseverance and passion. The impact of his mentorship is evident in the increasing number of French players making their mark in international competitions, further solidifying France's reputation as a powerhouse in the eSports arena.

The Evolution of eSports in Europe

kioShiMa's career coincided with a transformative period in the evolution of eSports, particularly in Europe. His contributions to CS:GO not only helped elevate the game but also played a significant role in the broader acceptance of eSports as a legitimate form of competition. As audiences grew and sponsorships increased, kioShiMa's prominence in the scene helped pave the way for future players, creating a sustainable ecosystem for competitive gaming.

Theories surrounding *cultural legitimacy* in sports suggest that the acceptance and recognition of a sport are often influenced by prominent figures within that domain. kioShiMa's success and visibility have contributed to the cultural legitimacy of eSports in Europe, encouraging mainstream media coverage and attracting significant investment. This shift has enabled the growth of tournaments, leagues, and organizations, fostering an environment where eSports can thrive.

Who Will Fill kioShiMa's Shoes?

As kioShiMa steps back from the professional scene, questions arise regarding who will carry the torch he has lit. His impact on the CS:GO community is profound, and the challenge lies in finding players who can embody the same spirit of innovation, teamwork, and resilience that he exemplified. The transition of legacy players into retirement often leaves a void that can be difficult to fill, as the unique combination of skills, personality, and leadership that kioShiMa brought to the game is rare.

The theory of *succession planning* in organizational behavior emphasizes the importance of preparing for leadership transitions. In the context of eSports, teams must not only identify potential successors but also cultivate an environment that fosters growth and development. As the next generation of players emerges, they will look to kioShiMa's career as a blueprint for success, and it is imperative that they learn from his journey to continue pushing the boundaries of what is possible in competitive gaming.

Conclusion

In reflecting on kioShiMa's impact, it is evident that his contributions extend far beyond the confines of the game. He has inspired countless individuals, redefined the role of support players, and played a pivotal role in the growth of eSports in Europe. As we celebrate his remarkable career, we are reminded of the indelible mark he has left on the CS:GO scene and the legacy that will continue to influence future generations of gamers. The journey of kioShiMa is a testament to the power of passion, teamwork, and the relentless pursuit of excellence in the world of eSports.

The Unseen Side of kioShiMa

Untold Personal Stories

In the world of competitive gaming, where the spotlight often shines brightest on the players' skills and achievements, the personal narratives that shape these athletes often remain hidden in the shadows. For kioShiMa, the French support player who rose to prominence in the CS:GO scene, his journey is woven with untold stories that reveal the human side of the esports phenomenon.

The Early Years

Born in a small town in France, kioShiMa, whose real name is Kevin Roux, grew up in an environment where traditional sports dominated the landscape. His parents, both avid sports enthusiasts, initially had dreams of him becoming a football star. However, it was the allure of video games that captured his imagination.

At the tender age of ten, he stumbled upon his first video game, a humble platformer that ignited a passion for gaming. This moment was pivotal; it marked the beginning of a journey that would lead him to the global stage of esports. The struggle between pursuing his dreams in gaming and adhering to his parents' expectations created a tension that would follow him throughout his career.

The Support System

One of the lesser-known aspects of kioShiMa's journey is the unwavering support from his family, particularly his older brother. While many players find themselves isolated, battling the pressures of competition alone, kioShiMa had a confidant who understood the nuances of the gaming world. His brother, a casual gamer himself, provided him with insights and encouragement, reminding him of the importance of resilience in the face of adversity.

This bond would prove crucial during the tumultuous times in his career, especially during roster changes and the subsequent fallout. The emotional toll of these events could have derailed kioShiMa's aspirations, yet the support from his family helped him navigate the complexities of professional gaming.

The Weight of Expectations

As kioShiMa transitioned from amateur to professional, the expectations began to mount. The pressure to perform not only came from fans and sponsors but also from within himself. The narrative of success in esports often overlooks the psychological burdens that players carry.

KioShiMa's experience is emblematic of a broader trend in esports, where mental health issues are often stigmatized. He faced anxiety and self-doubt, particularly during critical matches where the stakes were high. The fear of letting down his teammates and fans weighed heavily on his shoulders, leading to sleepless nights and moments of introspection.

To cope with these pressures, kioShiMa sought solace in meditation and mindfulness practices. By focusing on the present moment, he was able to alleviate some of the burdens he carried. This personal story serves as a reminder that even the most successful athletes are human, grappling with their own demons behind the scenes.

The Power of Community

Another untold story in kioShiMa's biography is the role of the gaming community in his development. The esports scene is often portrayed as cutthroat, yet it is also a space where camaraderie thrives. KioShiMa found friendships that transcended competition, forming bonds with fellow players that would last a lifetime.

During his time with Team EnVyUs, he developed a close friendship with fellow teammate, Happy. Their synergy on the battlefield translated into a deep mutual respect off it. These relationships provided a support network that helped kioShiMa navigate the highs and lows of competitive gaming. The shared experiences of victories and defeats fostered a sense of belonging that many players crave.

The Human Behind the Gamer

In the final chapters of his career, kioShiMa became an advocate for mental health awareness within the esports community. He began to share his story openly, shedding light on the struggles he faced and encouraging others to seek help when needed. This transformation from a player focused solely on competition to one who champions mental health reflects a broader shift in the gaming community.

KioShiMa's journey is a testament to the fact that behind every esports athlete lies a complex individual with dreams, fears, and stories that deserve to be told. His narrative is not just about the glory of victory but also about the resilience required to overcome personal challenges.

As we reflect on kioShiMa's impact, it is crucial to recognize that the untold stories of athletes contribute to the rich tapestry of esports. They remind us that while the games may be played on digital battlegrounds, the human experience is at the heart of it all.

In conclusion, the untold personal stories of kioShiMa reveal the depth of his character and the struggles he faced. They serve as a reminder that every player in the esports arena is not just a competitor but a person with a unique journey, deserving of recognition and understanding. Through his experiences, kioShiMa has not only shaped the CS:GO scene but has also left an indelible mark on the narrative of esports as a whole.

Insights from Family and Friends

In the world of eSports, the spotlight often shines brightly on the players, but behind every successful athlete lies a network of support, love, and shared experiences. For kioShiMa, the insights from family and friends reveal a tapestry of influence that has shaped him both as a player and as a person. These perspectives not only shed light on his journey but also highlight the human side of a figure often depicted solely through the lens of competition.

The Family Perspective

A Supportive Foundation KioShiMa's family played a pivotal role in his early gaming years. His parents, recognizing his passion for video games, encouraged him to pursue his interests while maintaining a balance with his education. "They always told me that gaming was fine, as long as I kept my grades up," kioShiMa recalls. This balance instilled in him a sense of responsibility and time management that would later serve him well in the high-stakes world of professional gaming.

Sacrifices and Understanding His family made sacrifices to support his burgeoning career. Late-night practice sessions and weekend tournaments were often met with understanding rather than frustration. His mother, in particular, would often stay up late, preparing meals for him and his teammates, ensuring they were well-fed and energized for long gaming sessions. "She believed in me before I even believed in myself," kioShiMa reflects. This unwavering support provided him with a safety net, allowing him to focus on honing his skills without the weight of financial or emotional burdens.

Friendship and Team Dynamics

The Role of Friends Friends played a crucial role in kioShiMa's development as a gamer. Many of his childhood friends were also passionate about gaming, creating an environment of camaraderie and competition. "We would spend hours playing together, pushing each other to improve," he reminisces. This collective growth fostered a spirit of teamwork that would become integral to his later success in professional settings.

The Importance of Trust In the world of eSports, trust is paramount. KoShiMa's friendships with teammates were built on mutual respect and understanding. "You have to know that your teammates have your back," he explains. This sentiment was particularly evident during challenging times, such as roster changes and losses in major tournaments. Friends within the gaming community served not only as teammates but also as emotional anchors, helping him navigate the highs and lows of competitive play.

Lessons Learned

Resilience and Growth Insights from family and friends reveal that resilience is a recurring theme in kioShiMa's life. His journey was not without its challenges, and the support network around him emphasized the importance of learning from setbacks. "Every loss is a lesson," his father would often say, a mantra that kioShiMa carried with him throughout his career. This perspective allowed him to approach failures not as dead ends but as stepping stones toward improvement.

The Power of Communication Communication emerged as another vital lesson from those close to him. In both family and friendship dynamics, open dialogue played a crucial role in resolving conflicts and fostering understanding. "We learned to talk things out, whether it was about strategies in-game or personal issues," kioShiMa shares. This principle of communication translated seamlessly into his professional life, where effective teamwork often hinges on the ability to express thoughts and feelings candidly.

The Human Behind the Gamer

Personal Stories Family and friends provide a glimpse into the personal life of kioShiMa, revealing the man behind the gamer. Stories of his kindness, humility, and humor paint a picture of someone who remains grounded despite fame. His friends recount moments of laughter and joy outside of gaming, highlighting his ability to connect with others on a personal level. "He's not just a player; he's a great friend," one teammate stated, emphasizing the importance of relationships in the eSports ecosystem.

The Impact of Community The community surrounding kioShiMa has also played a significant role in his life. Fans, fellow gamers, and mentors have contributed to his growth, offering support and encouragement throughout his career. "The community has been my backbone," he acknowledges. This sense of belonging has not only fueled his passion for gaming but has also reinforced the idea that success is a collective effort, rooted in shared experiences and mutual support.

Conclusion

The insights from kioShiMa's family and friends underscore the importance of a strong support system in achieving success. Their stories highlight the sacrifices, lessons, and love that have shaped him into the player and person he is today. In a world often focused on individual achievements, kioShiMa's journey serves as a poignant reminder that behind every champion lies a network of unwavering support, fostering resilience, growth, and the pursuit of excellence. As he looks to the future, the lessons learned from those closest to him will undoubtedly continue to guide his path, both in and out of the gaming arena.

The Human Behind the eSports Athlete

In the world of eSports, where the spotlight often shines brightly on the achievements and skills of the players, it is easy to forget that behind every avatar lies a complex individual with dreams, struggles, and a life that extends beyond the confines of a gaming chair. For kioShiMa, the journey through the competitive landscape of CS:GO has been marked not only by triumphs but also by personal challenges that shaped him into the player and person he is today.

The Duality of Identity

At the heart of kioShiMa's story is the duality of identity that many eSports athletes face. On one hand, there is the public persona — the skilled player, the strategist, the champion. On the other hand, there is the private individual, grappling with the weight of expectations, the pressures of performance, and the desire for personal fulfillment. This duality can lead to a profound internal conflict, as the athlete navigates the demands of fame while seeking authenticity in a world that often prioritizes results over well-being.

The Weight of Expectations

The expectations placed on professional gamers can be overwhelming. For kioShiMa, the pressure to perform was not merely about winning matches but also about representing a community. As a French player, he carried the hopes of a nation that had begun to embrace eSports as a legitimate form of competition. The burden of these expectations manifested in various forms, from anxiety before major tournaments to the relentless scrutiny of fans and critics alike. In many instances, this pressure can lead to burnout, a phenomenon that has been documented in various sports and competitive fields.

$$\text{Burnout} = \frac{\text{Stress} \times \text{Expectations}}{\text{Support}} \qquad (48)$$

Here, we can see that as stress and expectations increase, without adequate support, the likelihood of experiencing burnout rises significantly. For kioShiMa, finding balance was crucial. He often turned to his teammates, family, and friends for support, emphasizing the importance of community in overcoming these challenges.

The Role of Support Networks

Support networks play a critical role in the lives of eSports athletes. For kioShiMa, his family provided a foundation of love and encouragement that helped him navigate the turbulent waters of professional gaming. His parents, who initially had reservations about his gaming career, grew to understand and appreciate the dedication and passion he poured into his craft. This transformation was not just a personal victory for kioShiMa; it also highlighted a broader shift in societal perceptions of gaming as a legitimate career path.

Moreover, friendships forged within the eSports community offered a sense of camaraderie that proved invaluable. Teammates became more than just colleagues; they became confidants who shared in the highs and lows of competitive life. The bond formed through shared experiences, both on and off the virtual battlefield, helped kioShiMa to maintain his mental health and resilience.

The Pursuit of Passion Beyond Gaming

As kioShiMa's career progressed, he began to explore passions outside of gaming. This exploration is crucial for athletes who often find their identities tightly interwoven with their performance. By engaging in hobbies such as music and art, kioShiMa was able to cultivate a sense of self that transcended the confines of the gaming world. This pursuit of passion is supported by research indicating that engaging in diverse interests can enhance creativity and reduce stress.

$$\text{Well-being} = \text{Passion} + \text{Community} + \text{Support} \qquad (49)$$

In this equation, we see how well-being is a product of pursuing passions, engaging with community, and receiving support. For kioShiMa, these elements combined to create a more balanced and fulfilling life, allowing him to approach his gaming career with renewed vigor and perspective.

The Legacy of Authenticity

Ultimately, kioShiMa's journey underscores the importance of authenticity in the world of eSports. As he navigated the complexities of professional gaming, he remained committed to being true to himself. This authenticity resonated with fans and aspiring gamers alike, inspiring a new generation to pursue their passions while staying grounded in their values.

In interviews, kioShiMa has often emphasized the importance of mental health and the need for players to take care of their well-being. His candid discussions about the struggles he faced have opened the door for more conversations around mental health in eSports, a topic that is becoming increasingly relevant as the industry continues to grow.

Conclusion

In conclusion, kioShiMa is not just a name in the annals of eSports history; he is a testament to the humanity that exists within the competitive realm. His story is one of resilience, community, and the relentless pursuit of passion. As we reflect on the legacy of kioShiMa, we are reminded that behind every athlete is a person navigating the complexities of life, deserving of recognition and respect not just for their skills but for their journey as a whole.

The Future of eSports

The Growing Popularity of CS:GO

The trajectory of *Counter-Strike: Global Offensive* (CS:GO) has been nothing short of meteoric since its release in 2012. What began as a mere update to the classic *Counter-Strike* franchise has evolved into a cultural phenomenon, captivating millions of players and viewers worldwide. In this section, we will explore the factors contributing to the growing popularity of CS:GO, analyze the challenges it faces, and provide examples that illustrate its impact on the esports landscape.

Factors Contributing to Popularity

Several key elements have propelled CS:GO to the forefront of competitive gaming:

- **Accessibility:** CS:GO is available on multiple platforms, including PC and consoles, making it accessible to a wide audience. The game is often discounted during sales, allowing new players to join the community at a low entry cost.

- **Engaging Gameplay:** The fundamental mechanics of CS:GO—team-based gameplay, strategic depth, and skill-based shooting—create an engaging experience for players. The balance between tactics and reflexes keeps players invested, as they can continuously improve their skills.

- **Strong Community:** The CS:GO community is vibrant, with countless forums, social media groups, and streaming platforms dedicated to discussions, strategies, and gameplay. This sense of community fosters a supportive environment for both new and veteran players.

- **Regular Updates:** Valve Corporation, the game's developer, consistently releases updates, patches, and new content, such as maps and skins. These updates keep the game fresh and encourage players to return regularly.

- **Esports Integration:** The rise of esports has significantly impacted CS:GO's popularity. High-stakes tournaments such as the Major Championships attract large audiences, both online and in-person, and provide players with the opportunity to showcase their skills on a global stage.

Challenges Facing CS:GO

Despite its success, CS:GO is not without challenges. The competitive landscape is ever-evolving, and several issues threaten the game's standing:

- **Cheating and Fair Play:** One of the most significant challenges is the prevalence of cheating. Players using hacks and cheats undermine the integrity of competitive play, leading to frustration among legitimate players. Valve has implemented measures such as the VAC (Valve Anti-Cheat) system, but the cat-and-mouse game between developers and cheaters continues.

- **Player Burnout:** The intense competition and pressure to perform can lead to player burnout. Many professional players face mental and physical exhaustion, which can affect their performance and longevity in the scene.

- **Market Saturation:** As more games enter the esports arena, CS:GO faces increased competition. New titles with innovative mechanics and engaging gameplay can draw players away, making it essential for CS:GO to evolve continually.

Examples of Impact

The impact of CS:GO on the esports scene is profound and multifaceted:

- **Major Tournaments:** Events like the ESL One and the Intel Extreme Masters have become staples in the esports calendar. For instance, the CS:GO Major Championships, such as the *ELEAGUE Major: Boston 2018*, drew over 1 million concurrent viewers, showcasing the game's immense popularity.

- **Influence on Other Titles:** CS:GO's success has influenced the design of other competitive shooters. Games like *Valorant* have adopted similar mechanics, emphasizing teamwork and strategy, further solidifying the importance of CS:GO as a benchmark in the genre.

- **Emergence of Content Creators:** The rise of popular streamers and content creators, such as Shroud and Ninja, has contributed to CS:GO's visibility. Their engaging gameplay and charismatic personalities attract new players and keep the community vibrant.

Conclusion

The growing popularity of CS:GO is a testament to its engaging gameplay, strong community, and integration into the esports ecosystem. While challenges such as cheating and player burnout persist, the game's adaptability and the continuous support from its developers and community ensure that it remains a dominant force in the competitive gaming landscape. As the esports industry evolves, CS:GO will undoubtedly continue to play a pivotal role, inspiring future generations of gamers and athletes alike.

The Next Generation of eSports Athletes

As the digital realm continues to expand, the next generation of eSports athletes is emerging, fueled by unprecedented access to technology and a rapidly evolving competitive landscape. These young players are not merely inheritors of a legacy; they are innovators, driven by a passion for gaming that transcends the mere act of play. They are the product of a world where eSports is not just a pastime but a viable career path, and they face unique challenges and opportunities in their quest for greatness.

The Landscape of Opportunity

The rise of platforms like Twitch and YouTube Gaming has democratized fame and success in eSports. Young players can showcase their skills to a global audience, gaining recognition and sponsorships without the traditional barriers that once limited access to professional circuits. The equation for success has shifted; it is no longer solely about talent but also about visibility and branding. The ability to cultivate a personal brand online can significantly influence a player's career trajectory.

$$\text{Success} = \text{Skill} \times \text{Visibility} \times \text{Branding} \tag{50}$$

This equation underscores the multifaceted nature of modern eSports success. Players must now hone not only their gameplay but also their social media presence, content creation skills, and marketing acumen. For instance, players like Tyler "Ninja" Blevins have leveraged their gaming prowess into mainstream celebrity, showcasing how personal branding can amplify success in eSports.

Challenges Faced by Aspiring Players

Despite the opportunities, the path to eSports stardom is fraught with challenges. The pressure to perform at a high level is immense, and the competition is fiercer than ever. Young athletes must navigate a landscape filled with distractions, including the lure of social media and the demands of streaming. Moreover, the mental health implications of constant scrutiny and competition cannot be understated.

$$\text{Mental Health} = \text{Pressure} + \text{Isolation} - \text{Support} \qquad (51)$$

This equation illustrates how the mental health of aspiring eSports athletes can be adversely affected by the pressures of performance and the isolation that often accompanies a career in gaming. Many young players experience burnout, anxiety, and depression, which can hinder their performance and overall well-being. It is essential for the industry to address these issues by fostering supportive environments and providing mental health resources.

The Role of Coaching and Development Programs

To combat these challenges, the importance of coaching and development programs cannot be overstated. Just as traditional sports athletes benefit from coaches who guide them through technical and psychological hurdles, eSports athletes require similar support systems. Organizations are increasingly recognizing the value of investing in player development, offering coaching that encompasses not just gameplay strategies but also mental resilience training.

$$\text{Player Development} = \text{Coaching} + \text{Mental Resilience} + \text{Team Dynamics} \qquad (52)$$

This holistic approach to player development is crucial for nurturing the next generation of eSports athletes. For example, teams like Team Liquid and Cloud9 have implemented comprehensive training programs that include physical fitness, mental health support, and teamwork exercises, ensuring that players are well-rounded and prepared for the rigors of professional competition.

Diversity and Inclusion in eSports

As the eSports landscape grows, so does the call for diversity and inclusion within the community. The next generation of eSports athletes is more diverse than ever, with players from various backgrounds and cultures bringing their unique perspectives and styles to the competitive arena. This shift is vital for the sustainability and growth of eSports as it allows for a richer tapestry of talent and creativity.

$$\text{Diversity} = \text{Representation} + \text{Opportunity} + \text{Community} \quad (53)$$

This equation emphasizes that diversity is not merely a checkbox but a fundamental component of a thriving eSports ecosystem. Organizations that prioritize inclusivity will not only attract a broader audience but also foster innovation and creativity within their teams. Initiatives aimed at supporting underrepresented groups in gaming are essential for creating a more equitable environment, ensuring that the next generation of eSports athletes can thrive regardless of their background.

The Future of eSports

Looking ahead, the future of eSports is bright, with technological advancements and increasing mainstream acceptance paving the way for unprecedented growth. The integration of virtual reality (VR) and augmented reality (AR) into competitive gaming will create new experiences and challenges for athletes. As these technologies evolve, players will need to adapt their skills and strategies, further pushing the boundaries of what is possible in eSports.

$$\text{Future Growth} = \text{Technology} + \text{Mainstream Acceptance} + \text{Innovation} \quad (54)$$

This equation reflects the dynamic nature of the eSports industry, where innovation will be key to attracting new audiences and retaining existing fans. The next generation of eSports athletes will be at the forefront of this evolution, shaping the future of competitive gaming and leaving an indelible mark on the industry.

In conclusion, the next generation of eSports athletes stands on the precipice of a new era, armed with opportunities and challenges that previous generations could only dream of. As they navigate this complex landscape, their resilience, creativity, and passion will define the future of eSports, ensuring that the legacy of pioneers like kioShiMa continues to inspire and motivate aspiring gamers around the world.

The Legacy of kioShiMa and the Future of French CS:GO

The legacy of kioShiMa is not merely a collection of statistics or a series of tournament victories; it is the embodiment of a transformative era in French eSports, particularly within the realm of *Counter-Strike: Global Offensive* (CS:GO). His journey reflects the trials and triumphs that have shaped the competitive landscape, and it serves as a beacon for aspiring gamers in France and beyond.

The Cultural Impact of kioShiMa

kioShiMa's influence extends far beyond his gameplay. He has become a cultural icon, representing the tenacity and skill of French players on the global stage. His innovative approach to support play has redefined the role, emphasizing the importance of teamwork and strategy over individual accolades. This paradigm shift is crucial in understanding the evolution of eSports, where collaboration often outweighs personal glory.

$$\text{Team Success} = f(\text{Individual Skill}, \text{Teamwork}, \text{Strategy}) \qquad (55)$$

Where: - Team Success is the overall performance of the team in tournaments. - Individual Skill represents the technical abilities of each player. - Teamwork denotes the synergy and communication among team members. - Strategy involves the tactical planning and execution during matches.

This equation illustrates that while individual skill is essential, it is the interplay of teamwork and strategy that often dictates the success of a team in high-stakes competitions.

Challenges in the French eSports Scene

Despite kioShiMa's successes, the French eSports scene faces significant challenges. The transition from amateur to professional levels can be fraught with obstacles, including a lack of infrastructure, funding, and support for emerging talent. Moreover, the pressure to perform at international levels can lead to burnout and mental health issues among players. As kioShiMa has shown, resilience is key to overcoming these hurdles.

- **Infrastructure:** The need for more training facilities and coaching staff to nurture young talent.

- **Funding:** Financial backing is crucial for teams to compete at the highest levels, yet many struggle to secure sponsorships.

- **Mental Health:** The psychological toll of competition can lead to burnout, emphasizing the need for mental health resources.

The Next Generation of French Gamers

kioShiMa's legacy serves as an inspiration for the next generation of French gamers. His journey emphasizes the importance of dedication, adaptability, and the willingness to learn from failures. Players such as *ZywOo* and *shox* have emerged, showcasing the potential that exists within the French scene. These players carry the torch lit by kioShiMa, striving to reach new heights while embodying the values he instilled in the community.

The Future of French CS:GO

Looking forward, the future of French CS:GO is both promising and uncertain. The competitive landscape is evolving rapidly, with new titles and genres vying for attention. However, kioShiMa's influence will undoubtedly shape the trajectory of French eSports. His emphasis on teamwork and strategic play will continue to resonate, encouraging players to prioritize collaboration over individualism.

Moreover, as the global eSports ecosystem expands, there is potential for French teams to re-establish dominance in international competitions. The lessons learned from kioShiMa's career can serve as a roadmap for upcoming teams, emphasizing the importance of adaptability, continuous improvement, and the cultivation of a supportive community.

$$\text{Future Success} = g(\text{Legacy of kioShiMa}, \text{Emerging Talent}, \text{Community Support}) \tag{56}$$

Where: - Future Success represents the potential achievements of French teams in upcoming tournaments. - Legacy of kioShiMa signifies the foundational principles he established within the scene. - Emerging Talent refers to the new players and teams that are rising through the ranks. - Community Support encompasses the backing from fans, organizations, and sponsors.

This equation underscores the interconnectedness of legacy, talent, and community in shaping the future of French CS:GO.

Conclusion

In conclusion, the legacy of kioShiMa is a testament to the power of perseverance, teamwork, and innovation in the world of eSports. As the French CS:GO scene looks to the future, it carries with it the indelible mark of a player who not only excelled but also inspired. The future may hold uncertainties, but with the foundation laid by kioShiMa, the next generation of gamers is poised to rise and carry forward the legacy of excellence that he has established.

Index

-doubt, 27, 56, 59, 83, 99
-up, 46, 54

ability, 8, 23–27, 31, 32, 43, 45–47, 54, 60, 63, 66, 68, 72, 74, 77, 81, 83, 84, 88, 89, 94, 96, 107
absence, 86
acceptance, 77, 97
access, 81, 107
acclaim, 46, 86
accomplishment, 69
account, 10
achievement, 47, 68
acquisition, 18
act, 7, 14, 107
acumen, 19, 91, 95, 107
adaptability, 28, 38, 44, 47, 55, 63, 68, 69, 107, 111
adaptation, 28, 67
addition, 76
adjustment, 28, 31
adoption, 90
adrenaline, 86
adversity, 11, 47, 49, 66, 68, 69, 79, 98
advocate, 89, 99
aftermath, 47

age, 98
aim, 49
air, 92
allure, 13, 98
alternative, 85
amateur, 20–25, 28, 59, 89, 92, 96, 99, 110
ambiguity, 62
ambition, 37
analysis, 23
Anders Ericsson, 18
anticipation, 48
anxiety, 30, 37, 42, 46, 56, 57, 59, 62, 99, 103, 108
appearance, 38
application, 40
approach, 8, 9, 28, 32, 35, 38, 41, 44, 54, 62, 63, 66, 72, 73, 75, 81, 87, 88, 104, 108, 110
arena, 7, 20, 22, 35, 38, 41, 50, 57, 66, 81, 86, 88, 93, 94, 100, 109
arousal, 59
art, 104
artifact, 10
ascent, 22, 24
Asia, 81
aspect, 30, 47, 48, 56, 72, 79

113

assertiveness, 29, 74
assessment, 23
athlete, 14, 21, 26, 28, 30, 32, 49, 63, 86, 88–90, 99, 100, 104
atmosphere, 32, 46, 48, 51, 68
attention, 7, 13, 19, 21, 23, 24, 27, 40, 111
audience, 5, 81, 91, 107, 109
authenticity, 104
avatar, 102
awareness, 40, 89, 99

back, 3, 21, 38, 47, 93, 97
backbone, 66, 72
backdrop, 13
background, 109
balance, 25, 34, 42, 54, 55, 57, 69, 103
balancing, 7, 14, 29, 30, 57, 73, 82
banner, 69
bar, 56, 81
battle, 3, 46
battlefield, 99, 103
beacon, 9, 66, 76, 89, 94, 96
beginning, 13, 26, 28, 36, 93, 98
being, 10, 20, 25, 29–31, 54, 61, 77, 86, 87, 89, 104, 108
belief, 65, 68
benchmark, 7, 84
benefit, 27, 108
biography, 10, 11, 99
birth, 38
blend, 7, 13, 15, 28, 48, 69, 91
blueprint, 41
bond, 84, 98, 103
boot, 76
bore, 19
brand, 38, 107
branding, 4, 107

breath, 47, 92
breathing, 58
brilliance, 70, 92
brink, 24, 47
brother, 13, 98
building, 28, 34, 37, 40
burden, 32, 55, 56, 103
burnout, 2, 10, 31, 34, 57, 79, 103, 107, 108, 110
buy, 48, 73

call, 72, 108
camaraderie, 10, 14, 15, 18, 40, 56, 68, 80, 86, 99, 103
capacity, 85
care, 10, 104
career, 9–11, 14, 16, 20, 22–24, 26–28, 30, 32, 35, 36, 47, 49, 55–57, 63, 66, 76, 77, 79, 84, 88, 92–94, 97–99, 103, 104, 107, 108, 111
case, 11, 31, 33, 54, 74
catalyst, 15, 43, 49, 79
celebration, 70, 93
celebrity, 107
chair, 102
challenge, 7, 29, 44, 82, 97
championship, 19, 34
chance, 49, 51, 92
change, 72, 85
channel, 60
chaos, 47, 56, 58
chapter, 21, 36, 49, 66, 84, 88
character, 14, 27, 49, 100
characteristic, 21
charity, 89
chasm, 56
cheating, 3, 107
checkbox, 109

Index

chemistry, 34, 35, 37, 46
child, 13, 15
childhood, 13, 14
choice, 86
clarity, 58, 74
clash, 48
close, 69, 84, 99
clutch, 25, 65
coaching, 37, 43, 66, 77, 85, 108
cohesion, 21, 34, 47, 67, 75, 76, 89
collaboration, 35, 38, 41, 68, 72, 73, 76, 110, 111
collection, 43
Cologne, 31
combination, 21, 24, 48, 97
commitment, 38, 40, 43, 45, 75, 77, 81, 88, 94, 96
communication, 23, 25, 36, 40–43, 49, 53, 54, 56, 62, 63, 67, 68, 72, 74, 75, 88, 89
community, 2, 3, 5, 7, 9, 11, 13, 14, 24, 28, 43, 56, 57, 68, 73, 77–79, 85–90, 93–97, 99, 103, 104, 107, 108, 111
companion, 59
comparison, 56
competition, 7, 10, 14, 15, 17, 20, 21, 24, 46, 54, 56, 57, 80, 82, 87, 90, 97–100, 103, 108
competitor, 100
complexity, 91
component, 63, 109
composition, 33
composure, 42, 46
concept, 11, 31, 42, 47, 48, 74, 75, 85
conclusion, 3, 5, 11, 15, 21, 24, 34, 36, 40, 48, 68, 70, 73, 75, 77, 79, 81, 88, 100, 104, 109, 111
confidant, 98
confidence, 19, 45, 54, 63, 65, 66, 77
conflict, 25, 36
confluence, 22
connection, 13, 14
constant, 7, 31, 34, 59, 108
contender, 43, 45, 50
content, 77, 85, 87, 107
context, 7
continuity, 11
contrast, 28, 81
control, 63, 67
convergence, 3
cooker, 46
coordination, 15, 45
core, 71
cornerstone, 67
correlation, 78
country, 41, 77, 94
craft, 84, 103
creation, 77, 85, 87, 107
creativity, 13, 104, 109
crisis, 10
crucible, 14, 20, 26, 48
CS, 45, 51
culmination, 24, 38, 43, 44, 48, 63, 68, 69, 92
cultivation, 9, 111
culture, 3, 18, 21, 25, 35, 56, 63, 72, 77, 90
curve, 27, 28
cutthroat, 99
cycle, 34

dance, 14, 92
data, 63, 75, 83
dawn, 38

day, 29
death, 25
debut, 38
decision, 48, 69, 84, 85
decline, 34, 59
dedication, 19, 24, 28, 36, 76–78, 81, 90, 92, 94, 96, 103
defeat, 14, 21, 42, 46, 47, 49, 56
degree, 74
demeanor, 67, 74, 92
depression, 108
depth, 13, 100
desire, 34, 85, 86
determination, 14, 19, 26, 36, 38, 68, 91
development, 16, 20, 54, 76, 79, 81, 85, 88, 99, 108
dialogue, 10, 21, 79
difference, 20
dilemma, 29, 84
disappointment, 56
discipline, 13, 29
discord, 31, 36, 50
discrepancy, 56
disorientation, 72
disparity, 81
display, 92
dive, 66
diversity, 2, 80, 108, 109
dollar, 5
dominance, 81, 82, 111
door, 104
doubt, 27, 56, 59, 83, 85, 99
downtime, 54
DrDisrespect, 85
dream, 38, 109
dust, 34
dynamic, 3, 40, 44, 57, 80, 109

economy, 72
ecosystem, 9, 81, 90, 97, 107, 109, 111
effectiveness, 63, 67
efficacy, 77
effort, 35, 66, 89
element, 55
elimination, 47
elite, 36, 51, 87
embrace, 43, 68, 103
emergence, 1, 3, 5, 9, 79
empathy, 29
emphasis, 73, 111
encouragement, 11, 56, 98, 103
end, 49, 84
endeavor, 11, 66
ending, 10, 93
endurance, 46
enemy, 67, 69, 72
energy, 91
engagement, 3, 7, 88–90
enjoyment, 28
entertainment, 13, 14, 59
entity, 68
environment, 7, 10, 19, 20, 25, 28, 29, 36, 43, 45, 46, 53, 55, 56, 59, 61, 62, 80, 91, 98, 109
equation, 16, 25, 27, 31, 34–38, 41, 42, 45, 54, 56, 63, 66, 69, 75, 78, 82, 85, 87–90, 104, 107–111
era, 10, 38, 48, 91, 109
essence, 10, 20, 27, 32, 75, 82, 88
establishment, 2, 3, 45, 80
ethos, 9
euphoria, 69
Europe, 80, 81, 97
event, 46, 66

Index

evolution, 1–3, 5, 7, 11, 30, 40, 89, 91, 97, 109, 110
example, 10, 23, 40, 54, 56, 80, 108
excellence, 5, 7, 22, 33, 38, 43, 55, 94, 98, 112
exception, 43, 53
excitement, 30
execution, 45
exercise, 58
exit, 42, 54
experience, 19, 27, 46–48, 66, 70, 92, 99, 100, 108
exploration, 88, 104
exposure, 23, 24, 76
eye, 15

fabric, 5, 13
face, 10, 11, 45, 47, 66, 83, 84, 98, 107
fact, 99
factor, 63
failure, 46, 47, 62
fallout, 98
fame, 9, 94, 107
family, 13, 29, 69, 98, 100, 103
fan, 55
fanbase, 33, 38
farewell, 93
fate, 47
fatigue, 31, 42
favor, 68
favorite, 2
fear, 27, 47, 54, 62, 99
feat, 47
feedback, 28, 36
fellow, 35, 93, 99
field, 73
figure, 10, 55–57, 68, 86, 100
final, 68, 69, 91–93, 99

fire, 14, 48
firsthand, 11
fitness, 58, 87, 108
fixing, 3
flair, 84
flow, 31, 47
fluidity, 44
fly, 72
focus, 21, 31, 47, 54, 58, 65
footage, 41, 65
football, 98
footing, 36
force, 38, 45, 107
forefront, 24, 73, 80, 105, 109
foresight, 69, 75, 95
form, 14, 24, 54, 63, 66, 97, 103
format, 46, 50
formation, 35, 36, 38
formula, 69, 72, 73
formulation, 20
forth, 21
fortitude, 20, 21, 27, 28, 30, 42, 49, 50, 61, 65, 66, 83
fortune, 94
foster, 15, 43, 54, 109
foundation, 14, 15, 43, 45, 47, 103, 112
fragility, 46
framework, 88
France, 13, 14, 76, 78, 90, 94, 96, 98
friendship, 99
fruit, 19
frustration, 54
fulfillment, 93
function, 54, 73
funding, 81, 110
future, 5, 7, 9, 11, 13, 19, 32, 33, 36, 38, 41, 45, 47, 49, 73, 75, 76, 79, 81, 82, 84–86, 88,

90, 95, 97, 98, 107, 109, 111
G2, 53
game, 22, 25, 28–30, 32, 35, 45–48, 53, 54, 59, 62, 63, 69, 72, 74, 80, 81, 83, 85, 88, 89, 91–93, 95, 97, 98, 106, 107
gameplay, 7, 9, 10, 13, 20–23, 27, 31, 37, 40, 41, 54, 65, 66, 72, 76, 81–83, 85, 89, 107, 108, 110
gamer, 14, 25, 29–31, 54, 90, 98
gaming, 1–3, 5, 7, 8, 10, 11, 13–15, 20, 21, 26, 28–34, 36–38, 45, 48, 49, 55–58, 66, 70, 73, 76, 77, 81, 84–90, 96–99, 102–105, 107–109
gateway, 14
gathering, 72
generation, 20, 43, 66, 68, 73, 77, 80, 82, 84, 86, 89, 93, 104, 107–109, 112
glimpse, 63
glitz, 10
glory, 34, 48, 91, 95, 100, 110
glow, 13
goal, 18, 37, 84
good, 23, 91
graph, 9
gratitude, 92
greatness, 15, 20, 38, 46, 76, 77, 84, 93, 107
grenade, 67
ground, 15
groundwork, 3, 11, 16, 19, 21, 26, 30, 32, 38
group, 36, 43, 46, 88

growth, 2, 5, 7, 14, 15, 22, 26, 30, 43, 45, 47, 49, 62, 70, 78, 79, 85, 88, 90, 95–97, 109
guide, 10, 108

hallmark, 27
hand, 15, 85
head, 42, 94
healing, 87
health, 2, 10, 32, 54, 58, 73, 77, 79, 87, 89, 99, 103, 104, 108, 110
heart, 41, 93, 96, 100
helm, 38
help, 99
heritage, 11
high, 8, 20, 23, 27, 28, 31, 32, 34, 38, 42, 45, 46, 48, 49, 55–57, 59, 63, 67–69, 74, 77, 79–81, 89, 92, 94, 96, 99, 108, 110
highlight, 41, 100
history, 34, 38, 86, 104
hobby, 81
home, 13, 91
homeland, 13
hope, 11, 28, 89, 93
host, 57
human, 11, 55, 57, 68, 90, 98–100
humanity, 104
humility, 92
hurdle, 35, 55

icon, 89, 110
idea, 28
identity, 11, 15, 26, 27, 32, 35, 65, 86
imagination, 98
imbalance, 54
immersion, 47

Index

impact, 3, 7, 9, 16, 34, 42, 46, 59, 62, 73, 77–79, 81, 82, 89, 90, 94, 97, 100, 106
importance, 7, 8, 10, 13, 14, 23, 28, 32, 36, 38, 42, 45, 47, 55, 66, 67, 69, 72, 77, 88, 98, 103, 104, 108, 110, 111
imposter, 85
improvement, 19, 34, 38, 111
inability, 54
inclination, 34
inclusion, 108
inclusivity, 109
incorporation, 63
increase, 9, 103
individual, 21, 23, 25, 27, 32, 34, 35, 37, 43, 45, 53, 56, 63, 65, 73, 79, 84, 88, 90, 94, 96, 99, 102, 110
individualism, 111
industry, 3, 5, 11, 23, 61, 85, 104, 107–109
influence, 9, 33, 76, 77, 79, 88–90, 96, 97, 100, 107, 110, 111
influx, 4
information, 8, 31, 47, 74
infrastructure, 79, 81, 110
initiator, 67
innovation, 5, 11, 13, 38, 81, 90, 97, 109, 111
inspiration, 11, 76, 77, 90, 94, 96
instability, 35, 46
instance, 19, 21, 23, 42, 53, 56, 62, 65, 67, 72, 74, 107
integration, 5, 35, 107
intel, 72
interaction, 15
interconnectedness, 111
interdependence, 74
interest, 23
internet, 13
interplay, 3, 14, 27, 30, 35, 54, 56, 110
interview, 92
introduction, 15
introspection, 49, 91, 99
investment, 3–5, 81
invitation, 24
isolation, 54, 56, 86, 108

journey, 5, 9, 11, 14–16, 20, 21, 24, 26, 28, 30, 32, 34–36, 38, 41, 43, 46–49, 53, 57, 59, 63, 66–70, 76, 79, 84, 88–90, 93, 94, 96, 98–100, 102, 104

Kevin, 13, 14
Kevin Rabier, 13
Kevin Roux, 98
kill, 25, 68, 69
knowledge, 85

lack, 34, 36, 54, 81, 110
landscape, 1, 3, 5, 7, 9, 11, 14, 20, 26, 28, 32–36, 41, 44, 45, 47, 55, 56, 61, 65, 77, 81, 82, 84, 85, 90, 98, 102, 106–109, 111
layer, 91
lead, 10, 24, 33, 34, 36, 37, 40, 42, 46, 54, 57, 66, 76, 78, 81, 83, 85, 86, 98, 103, 110
leader, 32
leadership, 10, 21, 38, 67, 88, 97
leap, 24
learning, 14, 15, 21, 22, 27, 28, 42, 47

legacy, 9, 11, 28, 30, 32, 35, 36, 45, 48, 49, 63, 68, 73, 76, 77, 79, 81, 84, 86, 88–90, 93, 95, 97, 104, 107, 109, 111, 112
legitimacy, 3
lens, 18, 19, 90, 100
lesson, 48
level, 23, 24, 31, 34, 38, 42, 67, 81, 95, 108
lie, 96
life, 11, 13–15, 25, 28–30, 36, 54, 57, 86–88, 93, 102–104
lifestyle, 25, 31
lifetime, 99
light, 20, 77, 99, 100
like, 10, 14, 25, 41, 45, 54, 56, 57, 61, 67, 76, 78, 85, 90, 107–109
likelihood, 103
limelight, 24, 86, 87, 90
line, 54, 57, 67
loss, 46, 49, 84, 86
love, 85, 93, 100, 103
loyalty, 33
luck, 24
lure, 108

machine, 31
mainstream, 79, 107
major, 9, 38, 46, 48, 54, 56, 59, 103
making, 11
management, 14, 29, 43
map, 63, 67
mark, 9, 14, 26, 28, 38, 73, 77, 90, 97, 100, 109, 111
marketing, 4, 107
mastery, 15

match, 3, 18, 21, 23, 27, 28, 47, 48, 51, 55, 63, 67, 68, 74, 92, 93, 95, 96
mean, 20
media, 30, 38, 56, 79, 89, 93, 107, 108
meditation, 58, 99
melting, 20, 80
member, 35, 50
memory, 11
mentorship, 77, 88
meta, 7
metric, 63
mettle, 48, 53
mid, 45, 63
middle, 32
milestone, 26
mindfulness, 42, 58, 99
mindset, 19, 28, 62
miscommunication, 54
mistake, 25
mix, 27, 92
model, 9, 42, 74, 76
modeling, 75
moment, 24, 28, 35, 47–49, 63, 66, 69, 89, 92, 95, 98, 99
momentum, 68
morale, 34, 46, 54
motivation, 60, 89
move, 31, 37
movement, 24, 38
music, 104
myriad, 41, 59, 84
mystery, 10

name, 98, 104
narrative, 7, 11, 49, 55, 86, 95, 99, 100
nation, 103

Index

nature, 31, 83, 87, 107, 109
necessity, 13, 73, 96
need, 10, 11, 31, 49, 76, 79, 85, 104
network, 99, 100
networking, 23, 24
newfound, 45, 63
niche, 20, 38, 90
night, 69
norm, 35
norming, 88
North America, 81
notice, 21
notion, 72
notoriety, 24
number, 9

obscurity, 20
occasion, 68
one, 3, 7, 14, 21, 45–47, 63, 68, 77, 86, 90, 92, 94, 99, 104
opponent, 23, 67
opportunity, 18, 22, 24, 49, 70, 85, 87
organization, 24, 27, 33, 35, 38
other, 23, 81, 82, 85
outcome, 42, 74, 96

pandemic, 91
paradigm, 73, 110
part, 5, 19, 30, 61, 89
participation, 18, 19, 23, 27, 40, 42
passion, 5, 11, 13, 14, 28, 29, 76, 77, 85, 94, 98, 103, 104, 107, 109
past, 1, 55
pastime, 3, 15, 107
path, 20, 32, 34, 37, 66, 68, 85, 103, 107, 108
patience, 35

peak, 31, 92
perception, 8, 30, 56
performance, 8, 10, 17, 18, 21, 23, 24, 28, 30, 31, 33, 34, 36, 42, 43, 45, 47, 55–57, 59–61, 63, 66, 67, 72, 81, 83, 89, 104, 108
period, 21, 27, 32, 33, 36, 45, 49, 97
perseverance, 5, 9, 13, 14, 24, 28, 90, 93, 111
person, 100, 102, 104
personality, 32, 97
perspective, 88, 104
phase, 20
phenomenon, 1, 3, 5, 81, 98, 103
phoenix, 68
pill, 47
pillar, 91
pinnacle, 37, 41, 48, 84
pioneer, 84
place, 27, 43, 51
plan, 72
planning, 45, 65
platform, 17, 18, 23, 27, 89
platformer, 98
play, 3, 5, 17, 21, 22, 42, 44, 47, 55, 65, 67, 72, 73, 81, 87, 88, 103, 107, 110, 111
player, 2, 8, 11, 13, 15, 16, 19–21, 23, 24, 26, 27, 31, 32, 34, 36, 42, 46, 47, 50, 59, 62, 65, 71–77, 81–83, 85, 89, 91, 93, 95, 98–100, 102, 103, 107, 108, 111
playing, 27, 28, 31, 77, 90
playstyle, 21, 23, 27, 32, 51, 53, 80, 92
point, 19, 23, 24, 30, 59, 65
popularity, 4, 107

portrayal, 56
position, 23, 47, 92, 95
positioning, 62, 72
post, 9, 87, 88, 93
posterity, 11
pot, 20, 80
potential, 4, 5, 14, 21, 23, 34, 36–38, 40, 45–47, 68, 79, 85, 88, 111
power, 5, 7, 24, 38, 66, 68, 76, 90, 93, 98, 111
powerhouse, 47
practice, 14, 18, 29, 31, 37, 40, 45, 54, 62, 89
praise, 65
precedent, 85
precipice, 109
precision, 45, 92
premier, 45
preparation, 38, 43, 45, 66
presence, 23, 30, 38, 44, 91, 94, 107
preservation, 11
pressure, 14, 17, 20, 21, 25, 27, 28, 30, 31, 34, 37, 41–43, 46, 47, 50, 53, 55, 56, 59–63, 66, 68, 69, 74, 77, 79, 81, 85, 87, 92, 96, 99, 103, 108, 110
pride, 77
principle, 18
prioritization, 14
process, 18, 23, 24, 40
product, 30, 45, 104, 107
profession, 10, 28
professional, 3, 5, 7, 10, 11, 14, 15, 20–33, 53–57, 59, 63, 84, 87, 89, 90, 92, 93, 95, 97–99, 103, 104, 107, 108, 110

profile, 90
prominence, 9, 97, 98
promise, 46
proof, 78
prowess, 22, 51, 63, 66, 107
psychologist, 18
psychology, 42, 46
public, 4, 10, 25, 30, 56, 63
purchasing, 73
purpose, 18, 87
pursuit, 5, 7, 14, 22, 23, 33, 38, 48, 55, 77, 98, 104

quality, 82
quest, 22, 107
question, 82, 84

ratio, 25, 83
readiness, 24
reality, 5, 14, 28, 34, 42, 56, 84
realization, 93
realm, 10, 14, 15, 22, 30, 59, 72, 76, 104, 107
recognition, 3, 20, 31, 78, 79, 81, 100, 104, 107
recovery, 66
redemption, 49
reflection, 47, 68, 84
regimen, 29, 42, 62
reinforcement, 66
reinvention, 84–86
relationship, 64, 66, 89
reminder, 49, 55, 57, 70, 84, 91, 93, 95, 99, 100
renaissance, 9, 24, 68
repetition, 18
representation, 2, 16, 77
reputation, 19, 20, 23, 48, 65
research, 41, 104

Index

reset, 58
reshuffling, 34
resilience, 10, 11, 19, 21, 25, 26, 32, 33, 36, 38, 41–43, 47, 48, 55, 60, 62, 63, 66, 68, 70, 76, 77, 84, 86, 88, 91, 94, 97, 98, 100, 103, 104, 108–110
resolution, 36
resolve, 28, 38, 47, 50
respect, 21, 99, 104
responsibility, 56
result, 24, 45, 49
resurgence, 65
retention, 81
retirement, 84, 86, 91, 92, 97
review, 65
revitalization, 33
reward, 69
rise, 2, 5, 7, 9, 11, 14, 22, 45, 46, 49, 68, 79, 82–84, 91, 107, 112
risk, 69
road, 27, 31
roadmap, 89, 111
roar, 10
role, 8, 9, 19, 20, 23, 27, 28, 31, 36, 40, 46, 47, 50, 56, 60, 62, 66, 67, 71–74, 76, 77, 81–83, 85–89, 91, 94, 95, 97, 99, 103, 107, 110
rollercoaster, 46, 69
room, 54
roster, 24, 27, 33–35, 48, 82, 88, 98
round, 21, 67–69, 72, 92
routine, 29, 30, 58
run, 73
rush, 14, 67, 86

s, 8–11, 13–16, 18–33, 35, 36, 40, 42–47, 49, 54–58, 60, 63, 65–69, 71–77, 79, 82–85, 88–100, 104, 106, 107, 110, 111
sacrifice, 69
sanctuary, 13
saving, 73
scale, 90
scenario, 91
scene, 7, 9, 11, 19–24, 26, 30, 32, 36, 38, 55, 61, 63, 68, 73, 76, 77, 79, 81, 86, 89, 95, 97–100, 106, 110, 111
school, 14
score, 49, 68, 69, 92
scouting, 23
screen, 13, 46, 69
scrutiny, 10, 25, 28, 34, 63, 103, 108
search, 83, 84
season, 69
second, 23, 47, 54, 69, 74, 96
section, 15, 22, 41, 57, 63
selection, 24
self, 10, 27, 56, 59, 77, 83, 99, 104
sense, 18, 32, 56, 65, 69, 77, 84, 87, 93, 96, 99, 103, 104
series, 24, 33, 47, 50, 51, 68, 92
set, 7, 22, 24, 25, 57, 62, 67, 81, 84, 85, 90
setback, 49, 70
setting, 28, 32, 36, 48, 56
shape, 13, 22, 26, 85, 98, 111
share, 99
sharing, 10, 89, 96
shift, 3, 28, 73, 83, 90, 99, 103, 109, 110
showcase, 17, 18, 27, 66, 107
showdown, 68

shuffle, 46
side, 57, 98, 100
sight, 67
signature, 92
significance, 11, 15, 41, 46
site, 67, 69
situation, 91
skill, 18, 20, 22–25, 27, 28, 30, 32, 34, 35, 37, 38, 42, 45, 46, 50, 61, 68, 78, 81, 84, 88, 96, 110
smoke, 21, 67, 92, 95
solace, 99
soul, 93
source, 11
space, 99
spectator, 2
specter, 46
speculation, 50
spirit, 43, 68, 73, 80, 86, 92, 93, 97
sponsorship, 81, 90
sport, 2
sportsmanship, 93
spotlight, 30, 84, 98, 100, 102
squad, 21, 72, 91
stability, 33, 34
staff, 37, 43, 66
stage, 24, 27, 28, 32, 36, 38, 41–44, 46–48, 66, 68, 77, 90, 93, 96, 98, 110
standing, 81, 106
star, 23, 27, 38, 41, 46, 82, 98
stardom, 108
start, 28
state, 42, 47, 63
statement, 31, 43
status, 3, 22, 36, 45, 50, 94
step, 24, 46, 83, 93
stigma, 35

sting, 14
stone, 19, 49
storm, 55
storming, 88
story, 5, 10, 66, 77, 90, 91, 95, 99, 104
storytelling, 11
strategizing, 14, 69
strategy, 15, 20, 21, 27, 30, 34, 35, 40, 58, 62, 67, 68, 71–73, 84, 95, 110
streak, 25
streaming, 85, 87, 108
strength, 32
stress, 31, 46, 54, 57, 58, 62, 103, 104
strife, 53, 66, 68
stroke, 24
structure, 44
struggle, 3, 55, 56, 81, 98
style, 21, 44, 72, 74
success, 8, 9, 19–22, 25–27, 30–34, 37, 38, 40, 41, 45, 46, 61, 63, 69, 73, 74, 76–79, 81, 83, 88, 90, 94, 96, 99, 106, 107, 110
successor, 83, 84
summary, 7, 28
summation, 9
support, 4, 8, 9, 14–16, 19, 21, 23, 25, 27, 28, 31, 32, 40, 41, 45–47, 50, 62, 65–67, 71–75, 79, 81, 82, 88, 89, 91, 95, 97–100, 103, 104, 107, 108, 110
supremacy, 46
sustainability, 3, 109
sweat, 69
sword, 37, 46, 55

Index 125

symbol, 28
syndrome, 85
synergy, 23, 31, 36, 37, 40, 41, 43, 45, 48, 63, 67, 74, 88, 99

t, 13
table, 24
tale, 34, 53
talent, 9, 20, 23, 24, 45, 48, 76, 79–81, 84, 107, 109–111
tapestry, 10, 13, 88, 90, 100, 109
task, 35
taste, 69, 70
team, 8, 9, 14, 19–21, 23–25, 27–38, 40–51, 53–57, 62, 63, 65–69, 71–76, 82, 83, 85, 88, 89, 91, 92, 94, 96, 110
teammate, 99
teamplay, 75, 76, 96
teamwork, 9, 13, 23, 26, 30, 32, 63, 66, 68, 70, 76, 84, 88, 90, 92, 96–98, 108, 110, 111
technology, 3, 5, 13, 107
tenacity, 110
tender, 98
tension, 25, 46–48, 69, 92, 98
tenure, 8
term, 21
territory, 88
test, 27, 28, 46, 47
testament, 5, 7, 21, 24, 36, 38, 61, 63, 65, 68, 69, 76, 90, 92–94, 96, 98, 99, 104, 107, 111
theory, 10, 18, 47, 48, 57, 69, 74, 77
therapy, 87
thing, 3
thinking, 9

thrill, 14, 15
tide, 21
tier, 30, 85
time, 5, 13, 14, 22, 26, 29, 36, 54, 69, 81, 88–90, 93, 99
timing, 72
title, 51
today, 102
toll, 21, 31, 34, 54, 87, 98
tone, 67
topic, 50, 104
torch, 97
tournament, 19–21, 38, 40, 46–49, 54, 66, 91, 92
town, 13, 98
traction, 3
trading, 21
tradition, 81
training, 25, 27, 37, 42, 62, 76, 81, 108
trait, 46
trajectory, 24, 33, 35, 47, 55, 66, 79, 107, 111
transformation, 1, 3, 60, 63, 86, 99, 103
transition, 21, 22, 24, 25, 28, 46, 87, 97, 110
travel, 25, 31
trend, 5, 9, 99
triumph, 19, 31, 43, 48, 53, 63, 68, 79
trophy, 69, 94
trust, 34, 35, 42, 72
Tuckman, 88
turmoil, 33
turning, 19, 30, 65

uncertainty, 84, 86
underperformance, 34, 56

understanding, 11, 21, 22, 25, 29, 32, 41, 56, 62, 63, 72, 73, 84, 92, 100, 110
unit, 35, 37, 41, 45, 82
unity, 32, 96
universe, 14
up, 13, 24, 46, 50, 54, 59, 66, 91, 98
usage, 8, 62, 63, 67, 72, 73
use, 63, 95
utility, 8, 62, 63, 66, 67, 72, 73, 92, 95

value, 48, 74, 108
variety, 71
victory, 19, 21, 23, 27, 42, 47, 49, 60, 65, 68–70, 78, 94, 100, 103
video, 3, 13–15, 98
view, 72
viewership, 90
vigor, 104
visibility, 22, 77, 89, 90, 107
vision, 37, 38
visualization, 42
vocabulary, 62
voice, 67
void, 97

vulnerability, 10

wall, 47
wave, 69
way, 3, 13, 26, 41, 45, 73, 93, 97
weaponry, 73
weight, 37, 46, 53–56, 84, 91, 92
well, 10, 24, 31, 43, 54, 61, 65, 77, 86, 87, 89, 104, 108
whirlwind, 27, 30
whole, 100, 104
will, 3, 9, 61, 68, 76, 77, 79, 81, 82, 84, 86, 90, 93, 97, 107, 109, 111
willingness, 23, 81
win, 31, 72
work, 13, 24, 27, 28, 36, 38, 54, 57, 68, 69, 96
world, 10, 11, 13, 14, 20, 22, 24, 28, 30, 33, 34, 36, 38, 41, 45, 48, 49, 54, 55, 57, 59, 63, 68, 70, 75, 77, 84, 98, 100, 102, 104, 107, 109, 111

year, 48
youth, 29, 77

zone, 59

Milton Keynes UK
Ingram Content Group UK Ltd.
UKHW022127051124
450708UK00015B/1218